Sew and Quilt Japanese Décor

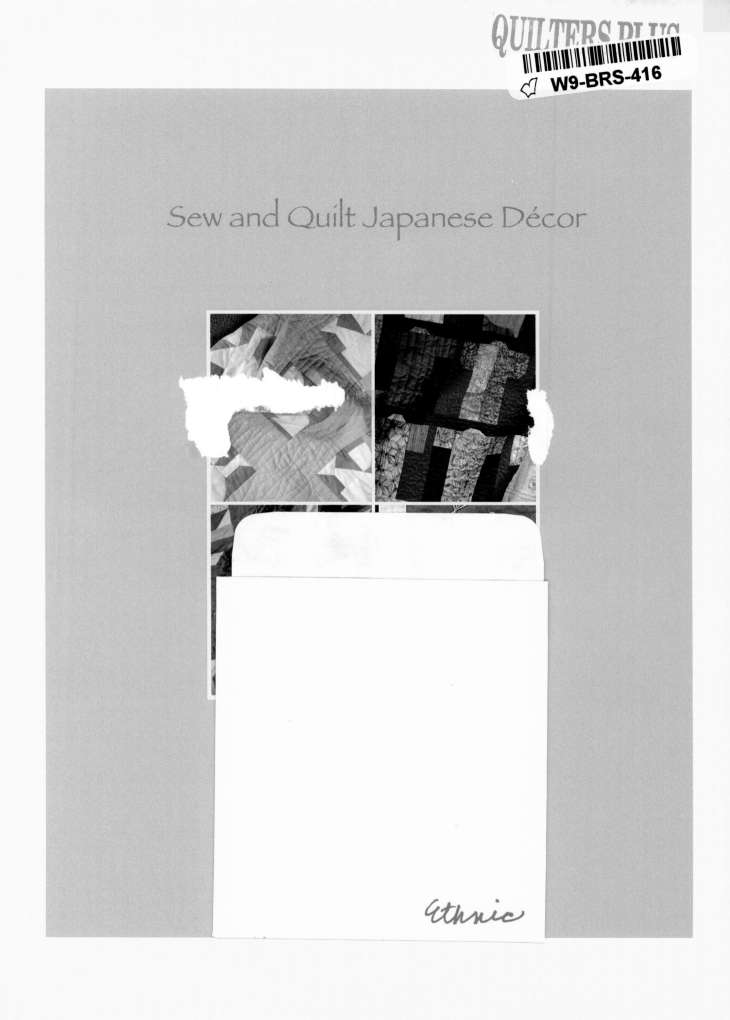

Ethnic

©2004 by Trice Boerens
Published by

 krause publications
An imprint of F+W Publications, Inc.

700 East State Street • Iola, WI 54990-0001
715-445-2214 • 888-457-2873
www.krause.com

Library of Congress Catalog Number: 2004100737
ISBN: 0-87349-784-8

Edited by Maria L. Turner

Printed in the United States of America

Table of Contents

Introduction

Unlike other styles of design, Japanese design can be clean and austere, while focusing great attention on the details. It is definitely an artistic dichotomy. Like the Zen philosophies that influence it, Japanese design is austere, but not rigid; abundant, but not florid.

Several years ago, due to a series of unexpected events, a teenage boy from Japan came to live with our family. His father wanted him to learn English and to temporarily live with an English-speaking family. In return for our hospitality, we would receive boxes from Japan that contained everything from jewelry boxes to plastic Godzilla figures, and there was always a confection thrown in for good measure. The edible gifts were usually tossed out because no one would eat the dried seaweed or the salted candy, but we would all marvel at the packaging. We saved every box, bag, and humble paper wrapper because each was so artistically designed. With beautiful graphics and clever closures, they became our curious and quirky treasures. It is said that tending to detail is an integral part of Asian life, from the wrapping of presents to the pouring of tea. I have the candy wrappers to prove that is true.

These details, combined with larger graceful lines and forms, are what attract me to Asian design. When studying art history, my favorite Van Gogh paintings were the ones with bold diagonals and Japanese script. My favorite Whistler portraits were those with the Japanese wallpapers behind the subjects.

Although I am a Japanophile, I don't claim to be an expert on the subject of Japanese decoration or design. So the projects offered in this book are not historical reproductions. Rather, they are colorful interpretations of popular techniques and themes—representations of Japanese sensibilities filtered through the eyes of a 40-something woman of Swedish descent.

Incorporating Japanese accents into a different style of interior gives a room an inviting feeling of exotic eclecticism. These accents add interest to mission, traditional, classic, and contemporary settings. Because of their diversity, the projects were photographed in a variety of room settings and styles.

General Instructions

Before You Begin

As you go through the projects in this book, there are several general points to know before you dive in and to keep in mind as you sew. They are:

- All measurements are given as width by length, except for those of strips used for borders.

- All projects are constructed with $1/4$" seam allowances. A $1/4$" seam allowance is added to templates for machine-pieced projects. No seam allowance is added to templates that are appliquéd or to hexagons that are hand-pieced.

- Before beginning a project, test each fabric for color fastness, especially those that are red. Reds have been known to bleed with as little water as steam from an iron. The Crane Quilt, the Fan Scroll, and the Peace Scroll, pages 28, 114, and 119 respectively, use hand-dyed fabrics. Launder the fabric after dying to ensure that it is colorfast.

- Some projects call for satin, moiré, and silk fabrics, but most of the fabric used is cotton. Choose a quality 100-percent cotton that feels soft and substantial to the touch. Inferior cottons or cotton blends don't hang or drape nicely, and more importantly, they don't feel good.

- Some projects call for small pieces of fabric that are considerably less than the size of a sheet of typing paper. The materials lists describe this size as a "scrap."

- When machine-piecing, trim threads often while working and then trim again when the project is finished.

Pinning and Basting

To secure two or more layers of fabric before stitching, use ordinary dressmaker pins or use basting stitches.

Pinning is the quicker alternative, but be careful when stitching over pins. Feed the pins slowly under the presser foot to avoid hitting them with the sewing machine needle, or remove the pins before they move under the presser foot.

Basting stitches are large over-under running stitches inserted by hand. Since they are temporary, it is not necessary to knot the ends when starting and stopping. Use a contrasting thread color to make the basting stitches easy to see and to remove.

Log Cabin Border

The log cabin design is one of the classic designs for quilt makers. The assembly process is adapted for a basic border.

Mitered Corner

When the corners of a border are mitered, they are joined at a 45-degree angle. The diagonal seams give the border the appearance of a picture frame. After stitching, clip the seam at the intersection and press flat.

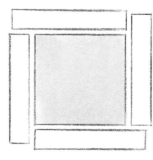

A log cabin block begins with a simple square. Then, strips of graduated lengths are added to all four sides to create a larger square.

Machine-Quilting

For a uniform quilting pattern, mark the quilt top with an air-soluble marking pen before layering with the batting and backing. Marks from an air-soluble pen fade slowly, until they disappear. There is no need to remove them.

Water-soluble pens are not recommended. Marks from a water-soluble pen require blotting to remove. Often, the moistened ink is absorbed by the batting and then reappears on the quilt top.

Here are some tips to know when machine-quilting:

- For a quilting pattern that follows the piecing pattern, or for parallel lines and/or free-form patterns, there is no need to mark the quilt top before quilting.

- Work from the center out.

- Use both hands to hold the areas around the stitching lines in place.

- Stitch at a slower speed than that of normal sewing.

- As you work, roll the quilt as it accumulates under the machine.

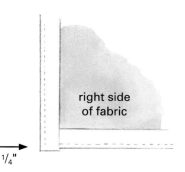

Stitch the strips to the quilt, starting and stopping ¼" from the corners.

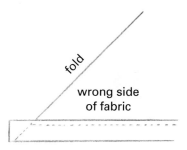

Fold the right sides of the adjacent strips together, align the seams and edges, and stitch together, using a seam at a 45-degree angle.

7

Binding

Binding finishes the edges of the quilt with a narrow, neat border. Here's how:

1. Trim the batting and backing even with the quilt top. Leave the first few inches of the binding unattached.

2. With the raw edges even, stitch the binding to the quilt top. At the corners, stop ¼" from the edges.

3. Fold the binding at a right angle, turn the quilt, realign the raw edge of the quilt with the raw edge of the binding, and continue stitching.

4. When returning to the starting point, fold the edge of the lower binding end under and overlap the opposite end.

5. Fold the binding around the raw edge of the quilt, and hand-stitch the remaining folded edge of the binding to the back of the quilt. At the corners, tuck the binding under at a diagonal fold.

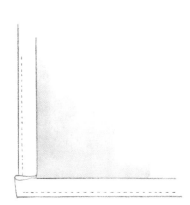

Binding gives the quilt edges a narrow, neat border.

Facing

Facing finishes the edges of the quilt with no visible border. Here's how:

1. Trim the batting and backing even with the quilt top.

2. Cut strips 3" to 4" wide and the same length as the quilt.

3. With right sides together and the raw edges even, stitch the strips to the sides of the quilt.

4. Press the strips away from the seam line, fold to the back of the quilt, and pin in place.

5. Turn the raw edge of the facing under and hand-stitch it to the quilt back.

6. Cut strips 3" longer than the width of the quilt.

7. Center and stitch the strips to the top and bottom of the quilt. Fold the ends of the strips in so that they are flush with the quilt sides.

8. Press the strips away from the seam line, fold to the back of the quilt, and pin in place.

9. Turn the raw edge of the facing under and hand-stitch it to the quilt back.

Embroidery Stitches

Buttonhole Stitch

1. Working from left to right, bring the thread from the back of the fabric up at 1.

2. Insert the needle at 2, and bring it back up at 3, while stitching over the first stitch.

3. Insert the needle at 4 and repeat.

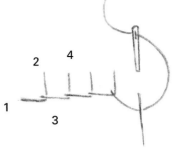
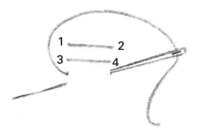

Buttonhole stitch.

Satin Stitch

1. Bring the needle from the back of the fabric up at 1.

2. Insert the needle at 2, making short, parallel stitches.

3. Repeat to cover desired area.

Satin stitch.

Running Stitch

1. Working from right to left, bring the needle up from the back of the fabric.

2. Make short over-under stitches, as shown.

Running stitch.

Needle-Turned Appliqué

Needle-turned appliqué is also known as hand-appliqué.

1. Before stitching, clip the seam allowance at all curves. Also clip inverted corners.

2. Noting the overlaps, pin the pieces in place.

3. Using a fine sharp needle and short lengths of thread, turn the design piece under at the marked line and then whipstitch the fold to the background fabric. Work in short distances of 1" to 2" and crease the fabric with your fingers at the marked line as you stitch.

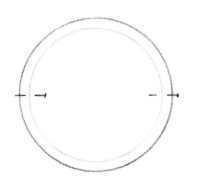

Draw around the shape with the air-soluble marking pen, cut around the shape, and pin in place.

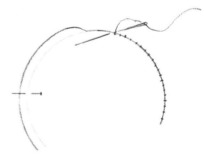

Turn the edge under at the marked line and secure with small, evenly spaced stitches. Remove the pins as you stitch..

CHAPTER 1

Flowers

Planting a flower garden is an act

of patience and of love.

It's the love for both friends and strangers

who will share in the joy of beautiful sights

and perfumed smells.

These flower-themed projects

also will be created with patience and love,

for which all those who enter

your home will be thankful in experiencing

their beauty.

Flower Garden Quilt

The word "Zen" means meditation. And since this life philosophy teaches that the universe has a spirit that permeates everything and every place, what better place to meditate than in a garden? The garden is regarded as a physical location that is designed to convey an abstract concept. Plants, rocks, and water are arranged to suggest such ideas as contemplation, gentleness, or dignity. The repetition of the flowers on this quilt suggests harmony and reassurance, both sentiments that are worthy of exemplification.

The real beauty of these flower quilt blocks is that they are easy to assemble because they are based on the traditional log cabin piecing technique. As in the log cabin tradition, this flower block begins with a square, the corners are trimmed to create a softer focal point or flower center, and then the graduated strips (leaves) are combined with small corner squares (stems) and are stitched to only two adjoining sides of the center square.

FINISHED SIZE: 57" SQUARE ■ SEAM ALLOWANCES: 1/4"

Materials Needed

1 yard gray cotton fabric

1 yard taupe print cotton fabric

1/2-yard light green cotton fabric

1/2-yard medium green cotton fabric

1/2-yard peach floral print cotton fabric

1/2-yard melon cotton fabric

1/2-yard cream cotton fabric

1/4-yard mauve/green print cotton fabric

1/4-yard dark green cotton fabric

1/4-yard olive green cotton fabric

1/4-yard burgundy cotton fabric

1 3/4 yards blue print cotton fabric

Tracing paper

Coordinating thread

Air-soluble marking pen

60" square cotton quilt batting

3 1/2 yards cotton fabric (backing)

6 3/4 yards 1/2"-wide blue bias binding

Cutting Plan

1. With the tracing paper, make the templates from the originals found on page 17. Broken lines indicate seam lines.

2. Cut the following:
   - 25 3 1/2" squares from the floral print fabric
   - 50 1 3/4" x 3 1/2" strips from the melon fabric
   - 25 1 3/4" squares from the burgundy fabric
   - 50 1 1/2" x 4 3/4" strips from the light green fabric
   - 25 1 1/2" x 5 3/4" strips from the medium green fabric
   - 50 1 1/2" x 6 3/4" strips from the cream fabric
   - 75 "A" triangles from the cream fabric
   - 39 1 1/2" squares from the dark green fabric
   - 36 1 1/2" squares from the olive green fabric
   - 25 "A" triangle from the mauve/green print fabric
   - 50 "B" triangles from the mauve/green print fabric
   - 52 "C" triangles from the taupe print fabric
   - 48 "C" triangles from the gray fabric
   - 4 3 3/4" x 58" strips from the blue print fabric

Flower Quilt Blocks

A finished block measures 10¼".

1. Referring to Figure 1-1, stitch one floral print square, one burgundy square, and two melon strips together. Press.

2. Referring to Figure 1-2, use the air-soluble marking pen to mark the wrong side of the pieced square. Trim ¼" from the marked line.

3. Stitch the long sides of three cream "A" triangles to the marked diagonal lines of the left, right, and bottom corners.

4. Stitch one mauve/green "A" triangle to the top corner. Press.

5. Referring to Figure 1-3, stitch three dark green squares, two light green strips, two medium green strips, and two cream strips to the pieced flower. Press.

6. Referring to Figure 1-4, use the air-soluble marking pen to mark the wrong side of the pieced square.

7. Stitch two mauve/green "B" triangles to the left and the right corners. Press.

8. Repeat steps 1 through 7 to make a total of 13 flower quilt blocks.

9. Repeat steps 1 through 7 again, but this time substituting the olive squares for the dark green squares in step 5, and make an additional 12 blocks for a total of 25 blocks.

10. Stitch the long sides of four taupe "C" triangles to the top, bottom, and sides of one flower block with a dark green "stem," as shown in the accompanying photo. Repeat for the remaining squares with dark green stems.

11. Repeat step 10, stitching the gray "C" triangles this time to the flower blocks with the olive green stems.

Figure 1-1

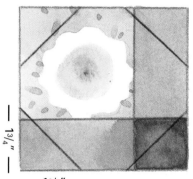

— 1¾"

1¾" *Figure 1-2*

Figure 1-3

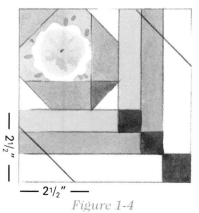

2½"

— 2½" —

Figure 1-4

Assembly

1. Alternating the blocks, stitch them together to make a grid of five across and five down. Press.

2. Starting and stopping 1/4" from each edge, stitch the four 3³/₄" x 58" blue print strips to the top, bottom, and sides of the quilt center.

3. Miter the corners, referring back to the instructions on page 7, if necessary. Press.

Quilting

1. As an option, mark the desired quilting lines on the quilt top with the marking pen. The machine-quilting on the project photo consists of curved lines within the flower and leaf shapes and stippling on the gray triangles.

Stitch the triangles to the top, bottom, and sides of one flower block with dark green stems.

2. Piece the backing fabric together to make a 60" square and press.

3. With the wrong-side up, place the backing fabric on the work surface. Carefully smooth out any folds and center the batting on top of the backing fabric. With the right-side up, center the quilt top on the quilt batting.

4. Secure all layers with pins or with long basting stitches.

5. Machine-quilt as desired, referring back to the instructions on page 7, if necessary.

6. Remove the pins or the basting stitches, and trim the thread ends, as well as the edge of the quilt.

7. Stitch the bias binding around the edge of the quilt, referring to the binding instructions on page 8, if needed.

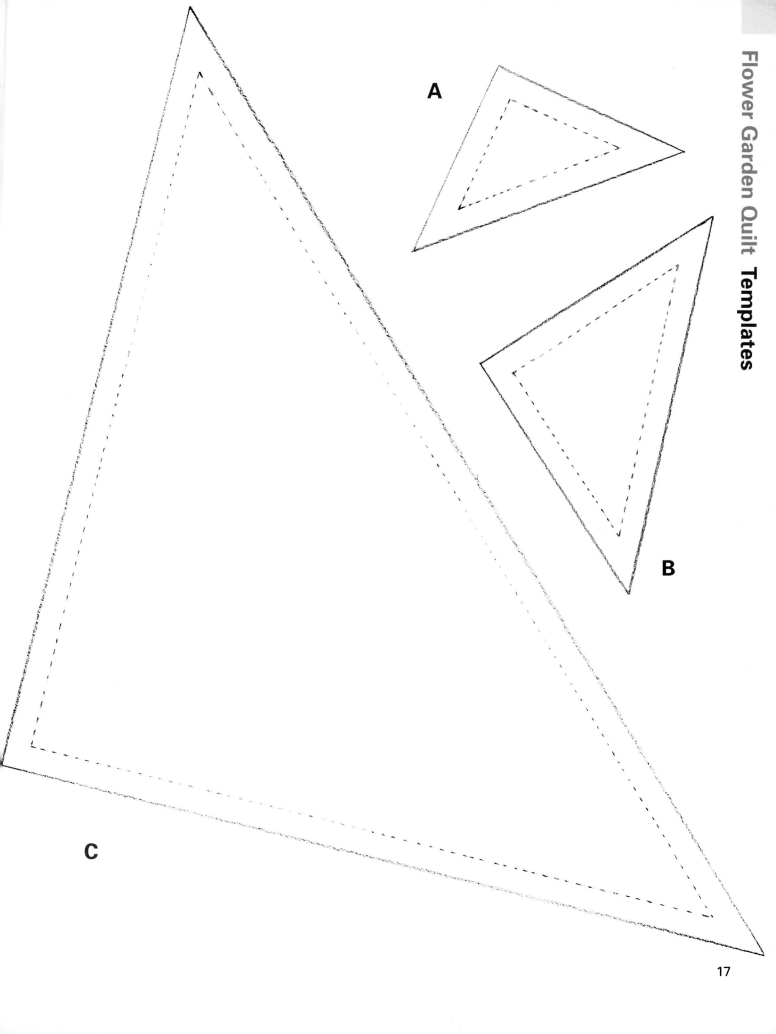

A

B

C

Peony Quilt

In the summer, peonies are in full bloom with rows of lush and ruffled petals. However, in the spring, they begin as stippled buds of color. Life is reborn in the spring and energy is found in evocative sights and sounds, with budding blossoms and singing birds marking the occasion of nature turning from gray to green. Since flowers are ephemeral, Japanese flower arranging is done with the character of the season in mind. Spring flower arrangements are simple and restrained with diagonal grasses or twigs added to suggest energy. This simplified version of the royal flower is arranged in a spare and ordered layout, complete with energetic diagonal lines. The peony is an ubiquitous motif in Japanese decoration. Painted on palace walls and stamped on formal robes, it comes in a close second to the chrysanthemum. The peony's vivid colors and fullness make it a symbol of riches and prosperity. With more than 30 variations, the orange version is called kinshi.

FINISHED SIZE: 53" SQUARE ■ SEAM ALLOWANCES: 1/4"

Materials Needed

1¾ yards cream multi-print cotton fabric

1¾ yards floral print cotton fabric

⅔-yard blue multi-print cotton fabric

⅔-yard peach print cotton fabric

½-yard pale yellow cotton fabric

¼-yard mint green cotton fabric

⅛-yard ivory print cotton fabric

⅛-yard pink print cotton fabric

⅛-yard green print cotton fabric

Embroidery floss, as follows:

- 1 skein blue
- 1 skein orange
- 1 skein green

Tracing paper

Coordinating thread

Air-soluble marking pen

57" square cotton quilt batting

3¼ yards cotton fabric (backing)

6 yards ½"-wide gold bias binding

Note: Like the flower block featured in the Flower Garden Quilt, the peony block starts with a log cabin square. The stem and leaf representations, though easily constructed, are more complex.

Cutting Plan

1. With the tracing paper, make the templates from the originals found on pages 24 and 25. Broken lines indicate seam lines.

2. Cut the following:
    - 8 2" squares from the ivory print fabric
    - 32 "A" triangles from the pink print fabric
    - 32 1⅜" x 3⅞" strips from the floral print fabric
    - 4 1½" x 50" strips from the floral print fabric
    - 16 "A" triangles from the pale yellow fabric
    - 16 1⅞" x 3⅝" strips from the pale yellow fabric
    - 8 "D" shapes from the pale yellow fabric
    - 8 reversed "D" shapes from the pale yellow fabric
    - 16 "C" leaves from the light green fabric
    - 8 "B" triangles from the light green fabric
    - 16 "C" leaves from the green print fabric
    - 12 "E" triangles from the peach print fabric
    - 12 "E" triangles from the blue multi-print fabric
    - 4 7¼" squares from the cream multi-print fabric
    - 4 7¼" x 48" strips from the cream multi-print fabric
    - 4 3½" x 56" strips from the cream multi-print fabric

Flower Quilt Blocks

A finished block measures 6³/₄".

1. Stitch the long sides of four pink "A" triangles to the sides of one ivory square and press.

2. Referring to Figure 1-5, stitch four floral print strips to all four sides of the square in a log cabin pattern. Go back to the Log Cabin Border instructions on page 7, if needed. Press.

3. Referring to Figure 1-6, use the air-soluble marking pen to mark the wrong side of the pieced square. Trim ¹/₄" from the marked line.

4. Rotate the square 90 degrees and stitch the long sides of two pale yellow "A" triangles to the diagonal corners of the top left and right corners.

5. Referring to Figure 1-7 and stopping ¹/₄" from the bottom edge, stitch two pale yellow strips to the sides of the pieced section.

6. Starting ¹/₄" from the top edge, stitch one light green leaf to one green print leaf.

7. To inset a "B" triangle, stitch one short side of a pale yellow "B" triangle to the diagonal side of a light green leaf, stopping at the seam. Realign the pieces and starting at the seam line, stitch the adjoining short side of one pale yellow "B" triangle to the diagonal side of a green print leaf, as in the making of the Crane Quilt Blocks, pages 30 through 32. Clip the fabric at the corners. Press.

8. Stitch the short side of another pale yellow "B" triangle to the bottom of the green print leaf. Press.

9. Repeat steps 6 through 8 to create a mirror-image pieced section.

10. Starting ¹/₄" from the top edge, stitch one pale yellow "D" shape to Figure 1-7 reverse "D" shape.

11. Referring to steps 7 and 8, inset one light green "B" triangle between the pale yellow "D" shapes. Press.

12. Referring to Figure 1-8 and starting ¹/₄" from the top edge, stitch the leaf sections to the bottom section.

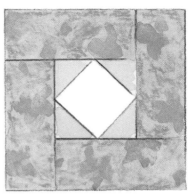
Figure 1-5

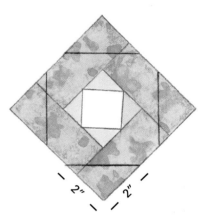
Figure 1-6

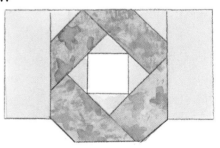
Figure 1-7

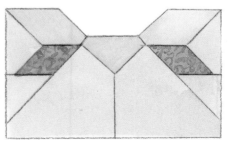
Figure 1-8

Complete the square.

13. Stitch the blossom section to the leaf-bottom section to complete the square, as shown. To join the angled pieces, match the edges, stitch to the seam, stop, realign the pieces and start again, as was done for the inset triangles. Clip at the corners. Press.

14. Referring to the photo, use the marking pen to draw a 1¹/₄"-wide circle centered in the ivory print circle.

15. With three strands of blue floss, stitch a running stitch around the marked circle.

16. With the orange floss, stitch a buttonhole stitch along the inside seams of the flower.

17. With the green floss, stitch a satin stitch along the center seam line. Stitch an "X" in the center of the circle, referring to the embroidery stitch instructions on page 9, if necessary.

18. Repeat steps 1 through 17 eight more times for a total of nine flower blocks.

Diagonal Quilt Blocks

A finished block measures 6³/₄".

1. Stitch the long side of one peach triangle to the long side of one blue triangle and press.

2. Repeat step 1 above 11 more times to make a total of 12 diagonal blocks.

Figure 1-9

Assembly

1. Referring to Figure 1-9, stitch the flower blocks, the diagonal blocks and the cream multi-print squares together. Press.

2. Starting and stopping ¼" from each edge, stitch the 7¼" x 48" cream multi-print strips to all four sides of the quilt center. Miter the corners, as instructed on page 7. Press.

3. Starting and stopping ¼" from each edge, stitch the floral print strips to all four sides of the quilt center. Miter the corners. Press.

4. Starting and stopping ¼" from each edge, stitch the 3½" x 56" cream multi-print strips to all four sides of the quilt center. Miter the corners. Press.

Quilting

1. As an option, mark the quilting lines on the quilt top with the marking pen. The project model shown is machine-quilted along the seam lines and within the blank areas. Since the seams serve as stitching guides and the irregular lines in the blank areas are free-form, the project model required no marked lines.

2. Piece the backing fabric together to make a 57" square. Press.

3. With the wrong-side up, place the backing fabric on the work surface. Carefully smooth out any folds and center the batting on top of the backing fabric. With the right-side up, center the quilt top on the batting.

4. Secure all layers with pins or with long basting stitches.

5. Machine-quilt as desired, referring to the instructions on page 7, if needed.

6. Remove the pins or the basting stitches, and trim the thread ends, as well as the edge of the quilt.

7. Stitch the bias binding around the edge of the quilt, referring to the binding instructions on page 8, if needed.

Templates

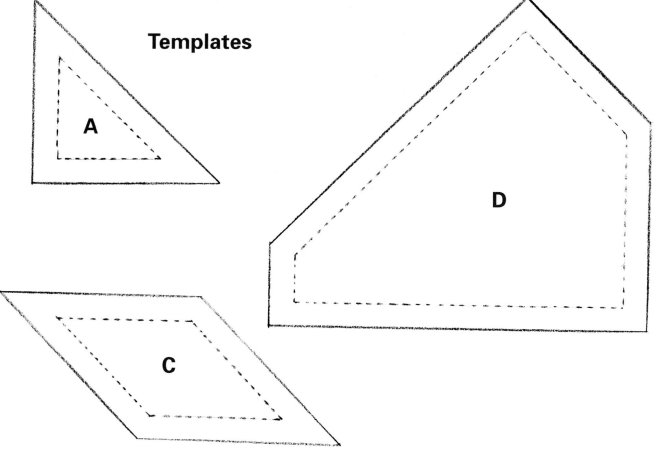

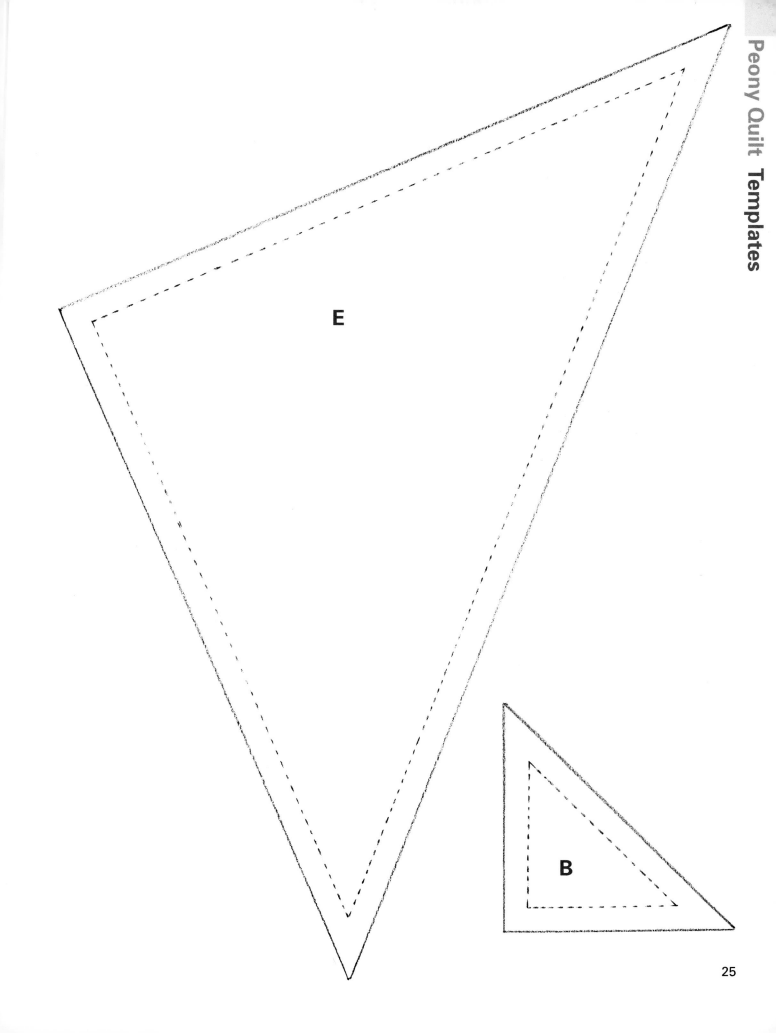

E

B

CHAPTER 2

Symbols

"The whole universe is but a storehouse of images to which the imagination will give a relative place and value."
—Charles Bandelaine,
1821-1867

Man is the only
creature on earth
who must create meaning.
When a beautiful form represents
a worthy ideal, its loveliness
is twofold.

Crane Quilt

The crane is one of the oldest bird species on earth, and the stark white Japanese crane is perhaps the most majestic. They fly south in the fall and return in the spring, and are associated with the passing of the seasons. Origami artists have been replicating these regal creatures for 300 years, using the purest of white paper. It is only recently that cranes have been folded with colored paper. Due to the pointed folds, an origami paper crane is very angular in appearance. By incorporating two curved seams in the fabric version, the appearance is dramatically softened and suggests movement or flight. The materials required to make this quilt include 1 yard of blue cotton fabric. In an effort to give the blocks an irregular and painterly quality, $1/2$-yard solid blue cotton fabric and $1/2$-yard of hand-dyed blue cotton fabric were used to make the project shown here. Cut the "sky" pattern pieces randomly from both.

FINISHED SIZE: 47" X 57" ■ SEAM ALLOWANCES: $1/4$"

Materials Needed

2 yards tan cotton fabric

1 yard white cotton fabric

1 yard blue cotton fabric

Coordinating thread

Tracing paper

Air-soluble marking pen

50" x 62" piece cotton quilt batting

3 yards cotton fabric (backing)

$6^{1}/_{3}$ yards white bias binding

Cutting Plan

1. With the tracing paper, make the templates from the originals found on pages 34 through 36. Broken lines indicate seam lines.

2. To simplify cutting and assembly, the block is divided into quadrants: the top left quadrant is the small wing; the top right quadrant is the neck and the head; the bottom left quadrant is the body and the tail; and the bottom right quadrant is the large wing. Refer to Figures 2-1 through 2-4 on page 32 to see the divisions. Cut as follows:
   - 20 each of shapes "B," "E," "F," "G," "J," "K," and "M" from the white fabric
   - 20 each of shapes "A," "C," "D," "H," "I," "L," "N," and "O" from the blue fabric
   - 16 7" x 5" rectangles from the tan fabric
   - 5 5" x 51" strips from the tan fabric
   - 2 5" x 49" strips from the tan fabric

Did You Know? According to legend, a crane will live for 1,000 years, and folding 1,000 origami cranes will please the gods. In return, the gods will grant a wish to the crane-maker. Thus, a proliferation of folded cranes now grace church foyers, school playgrounds, and community parks as a symbol of our worldwide wish for peace.

Crane Quilt Blocks

A finished block measures $6^{1}/_{2}$".

1. After cutting the curved shapes "B," "C," "M," and "N," trim $^{1}/_{4}$" from the perimeter of each paper template.

2. Center the trimmed templates on the cut fabric shapes and with the air-soluble marking pen, trace around the templates for seam guides. Mark the right side of the convex "C" piece (white) and the wrong side of the concave "B" piece (blue).

3. On the concave "B" shape, cut notches to the seam lines, as shown in the top left photo on the facing page.

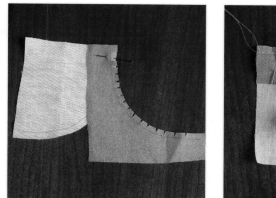

Step 3: Cut notches to the seam line on the "B" shape.

Step 4: Pin and stitch together the two shapes, rotating the "B" piece to match the "C" piece as you go.

Step 5: Stitch "F" to "H" and then the "G" triangle to "F."

Step 6: Stitch "G" to "H" to complete the triangle inset.

4. With the blue "B" shape on top of the white "C" shape, match the marked lines, pin the shapes together at the beginning of the seam, and stitch together, while rotating the top piece to match the marked line of the bottom piece as you go, as indicated in the photos above.

5. To inset the corner "G" shape, start the seam that connects "F" to "H" $1/4$" from the top, as shown above left. Stitch "G" to "F," stopping at the seam.

6. Realign the pieces and match the seam line of "G" to the seam line of "H." Stitch "G" to "H," starting at the seam connecting "F" to "H," as shown above right. Clip the fabric at the corners. Press.

7. Use the same technique as in steps 7 and 8 to inset shape "L."

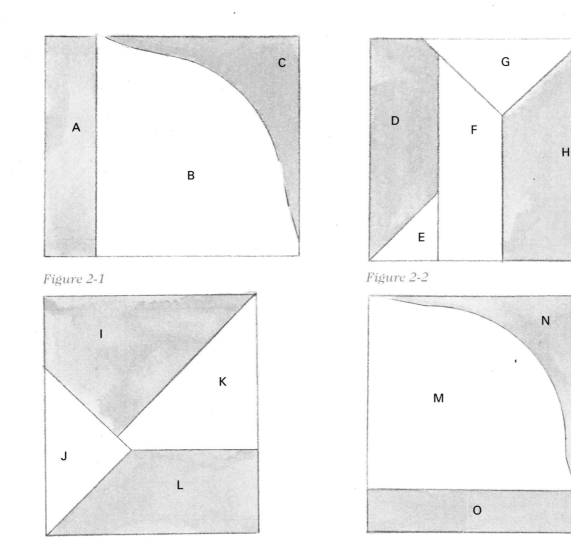

Figure 2-1

Figure 2-2

Figure 2-3

Figure 2-4

8. To make the small wing, stitch together shapes "A," "B," and "C," as shown in Figure 2-1. Press.

9. To make the neck-head, as shown in Figure 2-2, stitch "D" to "E." Then, starting $\frac{1}{4}$" from the top of the seam, stitch "F" to "H." Stitch "G" to "F-H." Clip the fabric at the corner. Stitch "D-E" to "F-G-H." Press.

10. To make the body-tail, as shown in Figure 2-3, stitch "I" to "K." Stopping $\frac{1}{4}$" from the bottom of the seam, stitch "J" to "I-K." Stitch "L" to "I-J-K." Clip the fabric at the corner. Press.

11. To make the large wing, refer to Figure 2-4 and stitch together shapes "M," "N," and "O."

12. Stitch quadrants together to complete the crane, as shown. Press.

13. Repeat steps 1 through 12 to make a total of 20 cranes.

Assembly

1. Alternating each, stitch five cranes to four 7" x 5" tan rectangles to make a vertical strip. Press. Repeat to make four of these vertical strips.

2. Stitch the three 5" x 51" tan strips between the pieced crane strips, as shown. Press.

3. Stitch the remaining two 5" x 51" tan strips to the sides of the quilt center. Press.

4. Stitch the two 5" x 49" tan strips to the top and the bottom of the quilt center. Press.

Finish the crane block.

Quilting

1. As an option, mark the desired quilting lines on the quilt top with the marking pen. The project model shown is machine-quilted along the seam lines and on the sashing. Since the seams serve as stitching guides and the irregular lines on the sashing are free-form, the photo model required no marked lines.

2. Piece the backing fabric together to make a 50" x 62" rectangle. Press.

3. With the wrong-side up, place the backing fabric on the work surface. Carefully smooth out any folds and center the batting on top of the backing fabric. With the right-side up, center the quilt top on the quilt batting.

4. Secure all layers with pins or with long basting stitches.

5. Machine-quilt as desired, referring to the instructions on page 7, if necessary.

6. Remove the pins or the basting stitches, trim the thread ends, and trim the edge of the quilt.

7. Stitch the bias binding around the edge of the quilt, referring to the binding instructions on page 8, if needed.

Stitch the tan pieces to the crane blocks.

Templates

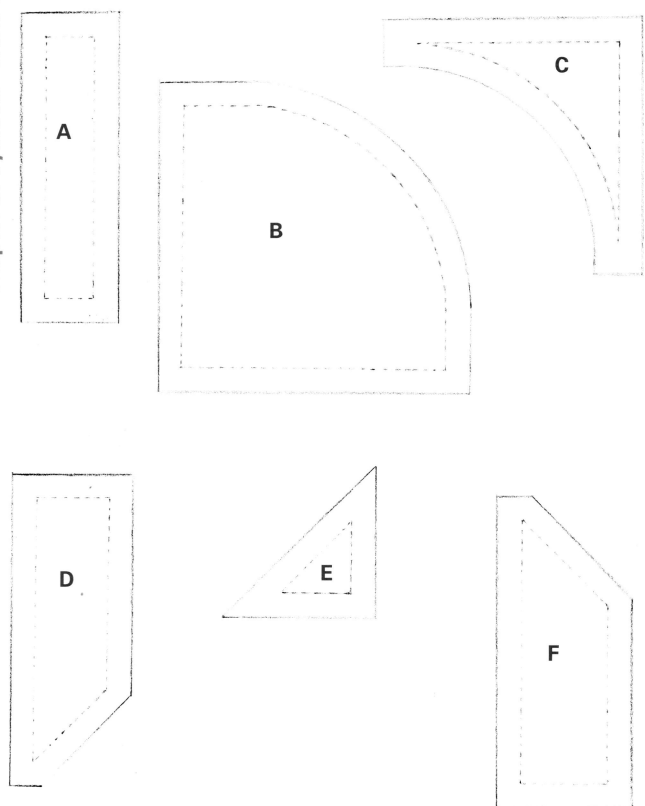

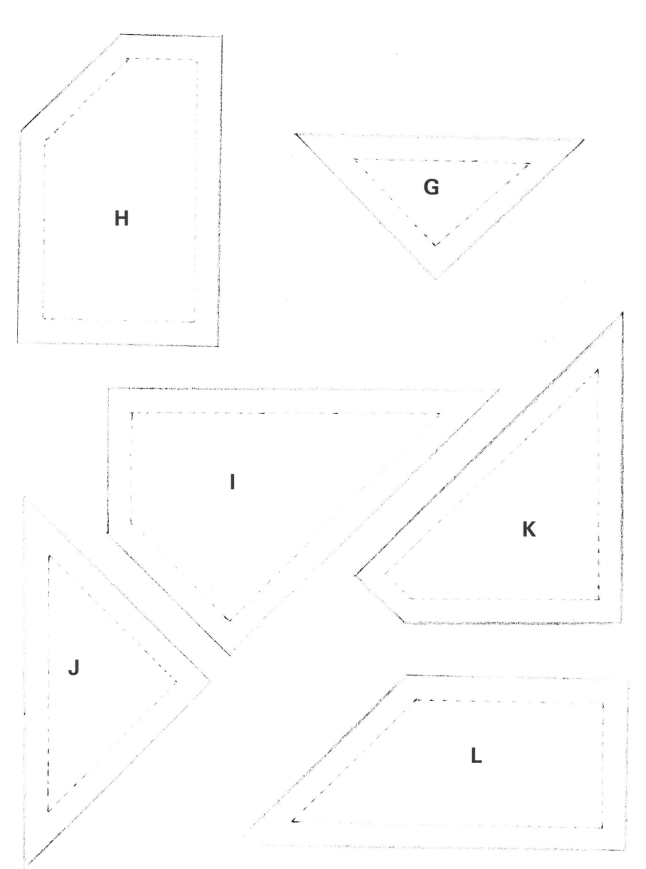

H

G

I

K

J

L

Templates

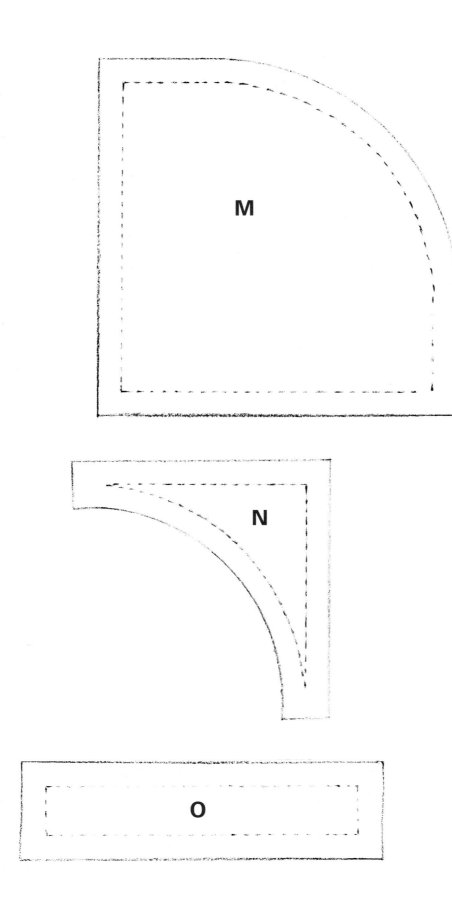

M

N

O

Cherries Pillow

During the eighth century, the Japanese emperor became so enamored with cherry blossoms—the symbol of beauty—that he ordered cherry trees to be planted around the palace grounds. Today, cherry trees grow in gardens throughout the country, and people gather in the groves for parties and celebrations.

FINISHED SIZE: 14" SQUARE ■ SEAM ALLOWANCES: ¹/₄"

Materials Needed

¼-yard light lavender print cotton fabric

¼-yard gray cotton fabric

⅛-yard medium lavender print cotton fabric

¼-yard purple print cotton fabric

Scraps of green cotton fabric (leaves)

Scraps of burgundy cotton fabric (cherries)

Tracing paper

Air-soluble marking pen

15" square muslin

15" square cotton quilt batting

Lavender machine embroidery thread

Coordinating thread (assembly)

15" square cotton fabric (pillow back)

14" pillow form

Cutting Plan

1. With the tracing paper, make the templates from the originals found on page 45. Broken lines indicate seam lines.

2. Cut the following:
   - 6 1⅞" squares from the burgundy fabric
   - 6 1¼" scraps from the lavender fabric
   - 2 1⅞" squares from the lavender fabric
   - 6 2¼" squares from the green fabric
   - 4 1½" x 2¼" rectangles from the light lavender print fabric
   - 4 "A" triangles from the light lavender print fabric
   - 4 "B" triangles from the light lavender print fabric
   - 2 5" squares from the light lavender print fabric
   - 2 1½" x 5" strips from the gray fabric
   - 1½" x 10½" strip from the gray fabric
   - 4 1¾" x 13" strips from the gray fabric
   - 2 1¼" x 13" strips from the medium lavender print fabric
   - 2 1¼" x 14½" strips from the medium lavender print fabric
   - 4 2½" x 14¼" strips from the purple print fabric

Cherry Blocks

A finished block measures 4½".

1. Referring to Figure 2-5, use the air-soluble marking pen to mark the wrong side of three 1⅞" burgundy squares.

2. Stitch the 1¼" lavender scraps to the marked diagonal lines of all four corners of the burgundy squares. Press. Trim the lavender corners to make 1⅞" squares.

3. Referring to Figure 2-6 at top left of facing page, stitch the squares together to create a cherries square. Press.

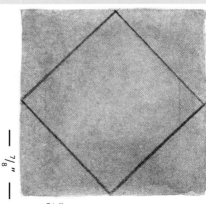

7/8"

— 7/8" —

Figure 2-5

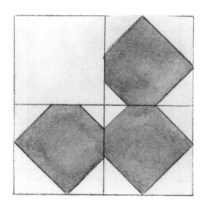

Figure 2-6

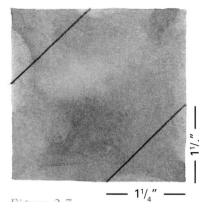

Figure 2-7

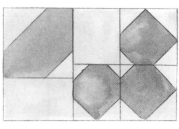

Figure 2-8

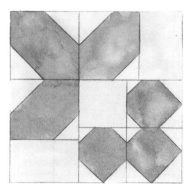

Figure 2-9

4. Referring to Figure 2-7, use the marking pen to mark the wrong side of three 2¹/₄" green squares.

5. Stitch one light lavender print "A" triangle to the marked diagonal line on one 2¹/₄" green square to create a leaf piece.

6. Repeat step 5 for the other two green squares.

7. Referring to Figure 2-8, stitch one light lavender print 1¹/₂" x 2¹/₄" rectangle and one leaf piece to the cherries square. Press.

8. Referring to Figure 2-9, stitch the remaining leaf pieces and lavender print rectangles together, as shown.

9. To inset the light lavender print "B" triangles between the leaves, stitch the short side of one "B" triangle to the diagonal side of the leaf stopping at the seam. Realign the pieces and stitch the remaining short side to the diagonal side of the second leaf to complete the block, as shown at right. Clip the fabric at the corners. Press.

10. Repeat steps 1 through 9 to make a second cherry block.

Pillow Top Assembly

1. Referring to the accompanying photo, stitch the 5" lavender print squares and the two 1¹/₂" x 5" gray strips, as well as the 1¹/₂" x 10¹/₂" gray strip, to the cherries blocks. Press.

2. Starting and stopping ¹/₄" from each edge, stitch each of the four 1³/₄" x 13" gray strips to all four sides of the pillow center. Miter the corners, as instructed on page 7. Press.

Complete the cherries block.

Stitch the gray strips, lavender squares, and cherries blocks together to create the pillow center.

3. Stitch the two 1¹⁄₄" x 13" medium lavender strips to the sides of the pillow center, and the two 1¹⁄₄" x 14¹⁄₂" medium lavender strips to the top and the bottom of the pillow center. Press.

Quilting

1. Place the muslin on the work surface, followed by the batting on the muslin, and then center the pillow top on the batting right-side up.

2. Secure all layers with pins or with basting stitches.

3. Machine-quilt around the squares and along the borders.

4. Referring to the photo at right, use the air-soluble marking pen to draw the stems on the pillow top.

5. On a scrap of fabric, machine satin stitch a short straight line. Adjust your machine to the desired line width and coverage. The width of the stems is ¹⁄₁₆".

6. With the lavender thread, stitch the stems through all layers. Trim the thread ends.

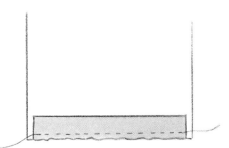

Draw the stems onto the block.

Figure 2-10

Pillow Assembly

1. With the wrong sides together, fold one 2¹⁄₂" x 14¹⁄₄" purple print strip in half lengthwise. Stitch them together at the short sides. Trim the excess fabric from the corners and turn right side out. Press. Repeat for remaining purple print strips.

2. Referring to Figure 2-10, match the raw edges, center, and baste a strip to the right side of the pillow top. Repeat with the remaining three strips.

3. With the right sides together, pin the pillow front to the pillow back.

4. Stitch together, leaving an 8" opening on one side.

5. Trim the excess fabric from the corners, turn right-side out, press, and insert the pillow form.

6. Whipstitch the opening closed.

Templates

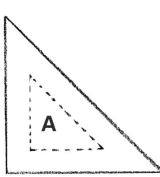

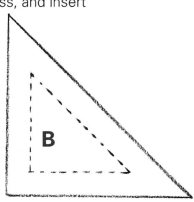

Dragonfly Pillow

The dragonfly is a natural marvel with two sets of wings that beat independently of each other. A dragonfly is the symbol of enlightenment. If a dragonfly lands on your shoulder, it is a great honor, like they are considered to bring light and joy.

FINISHED SIZE: 14" SQUARE ■ SEAM ALLOWANCES: ¼"

Materials Needed

$1/4$-yard dark red cotton fabric

$1/4$-yard dark pink print cotton fabric

$1/4$-yard white cotton fabric

$1/8$-yard purple print cotton fabric

Scraps of cotton fabric in the following colors (dragonfly):

- tan
- light green
- light blue print

Tracing paper

Air-soluble marking pen

15" square muslin

15" square cotton quilt batting

Coordinating thread (assembly)

15" square cotton fabric (pillow back)

14" pillow form

Cutting Plan

1. With the tracing paper, make the templates from the originals found on page 45. Broken lines indicate seam lines.

2. Cut the following:
    - 2 1" x $1^{1}/_{4}$" rectangles from the dark red fabric
    - 2" x $2^{1}/_{2}$" rectangle from the dark red fabric
    - $2^{1}/_{2}$" x 4" rectangle from the dark red fabric
    - 2 "A" triangles from the dark red fabric
    - 2 "C" shapes from the dark red fabric
    - 2 "E" triangles from the dark red fabric
    - 2 $1^{1}/_{2}$" x 4" strips from the dark red fabric
    - $5^{1}/_{8}$" square from the dark red fabric
    - 2 $3/_{4}$" x $1^{1}/_{4}$" rectangles from the tan fabric
    - $1^{1}/_{4}$" square from the tan fabric
    - $7/_{8}$" x 7" strip from the tan fabric
    - $1^{1}/_{2}$" square from the tan fabric
    - $1^{1}/_{4}$" square from the light green fabric
    - "B" shape from the light green fabric
    - reverse "B" shape from light green fabric*
    - "D" shape from the light blue fabric
    - reverse "D" shape from the light blue fabric*
    - 4 $1^{1}/_{2}$" x $9^{1}/_{2}$" strips from the white fabric
    - 4 2" x 13" strips from the white fabric
    - 4 1" x 11" strips from the purple print fabric
    - 4 $2^{1}/_{2}$" x $14^{1}/_{4}$" strips from the dark pink print fabric

*Reverse the templates to create mirror-image shapes.

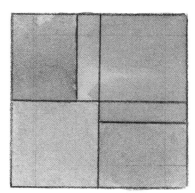

Figure 2-11

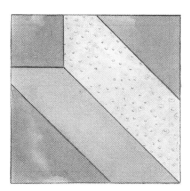

Figure 2-12

Figure 2-13

Dragonfly Block

A finished block measures 8".

1. Referring to Figure 2-11, stitch together the two 1" x 1$\frac{1}{4}$" dark red rectangles, two $\frac{3}{4}$" x 1$\frac{1}{4}$" tan rectangles, one 1$\frac{1}{4}$" tan square, and one 1$\frac{1}{4}$" green square. Press.

2. Stitch the short side of the 2" x 2$\frac{1}{2}$" dark red rectangle to the top of the pieced square.

3. Stitch the long side of the 2$\frac{1}{2}$" x 4" dark red rectangle to the pieced rectangle. Press.

Figure 2-14

4. Referring to Figure 2-12, stitch together one dark red "A" triangle, the light green "B" shape, the light blue print "D" shape, and one dark red "E" triangle.

5. To inset the dark red "C" shape, stitch the wings together, starting $\frac{1}{4}$" from the top edge. Stitch one side of the square to the top of the green wing stopping at the seam. Realign the pieces and stitch the adjoining side of the square to the side of the light blue wing.
   Clip the fabric at the corner. Press.

6. Stitch one 1$\frac{1}{2}$" x 4" dark red strip to the left side of the pieced square. Press.

7. Repeat steps 4 through 6, this time using the light green reverse "B" and light blue reverse "D" shapes.

8. Cut the dark red 5$\frac{1}{8}$" square in half diagonally.

9. Stitch the $\frac{7}{8}$" x 7" tan strip between the long sides of the dark red triangles from step 8 to re-create a square. Press.

10. Referring to Figure 2-13, use the air-soluble marking pen to mark the seam lines on the 1$\frac{1}{2}$" tan square.

11. Referring to Figure 2-14, trim the fabric and then clip the fabric to the marked corner.

12. To inset the square, match one side of the square to the marked line and stitch to the clipped corner. Realign the pieces and stitch the adjoining side of the square to the remaining marked line. Press.

13. Referring to the photo at right, stitch the four sections together to complete the square. Press.

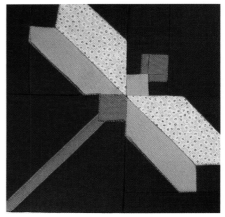

Stitch the blocks together to form the pillow center.

Pillow Top Assembly

1. Stitch each of the 1$\frac{1}{2}$" x 9$\frac{1}{2}$" white strips to each side of the dragonfly pillow center in a log cabin pattern, as detailed in the border instructions on page 7. Press.

2. Stitch the 1" x 11" purple print strips to the pillow center in a log cabin pattern. Press.

3. Stitch the 2" x 13" white strips to the pillow center in a log cabin pattern. Press.

Quilting

1. Place the muslin on the work surface, followed by the batting on the muslin, and then center the pillow top on the batting right-side up.

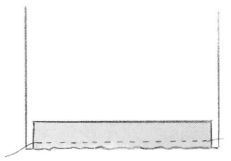

Figure 2-15

2. Secure all layers with pins or with basting stitches.

3. Machine-quilt around the dragonfly and along the borders.

Pillow Assembly

1. With the wrong sides together, fold one 2$\frac{1}{2}$" x 14$\frac{1}{4}$" dark pink strip in half lengthwise. Stitch them together at the short sides. Trim the excess fabric from the corners and turn right-side out. Press. Repeat for the remaining dark pink strips.

2. Referring to Figure 2-15, match the raw edges, center, and baste a strip to the right side of the pillow top. Repeat with the remaining three strips.

3. With the right sides together, pin the pillow front to the pillow back.

4. Stitch together, leaving an 8" opening on one side.

5. Trim the excess fabric from the corners, turn right-side out, press, and insert the pillow form.

6. Whipstitch the opening closed.

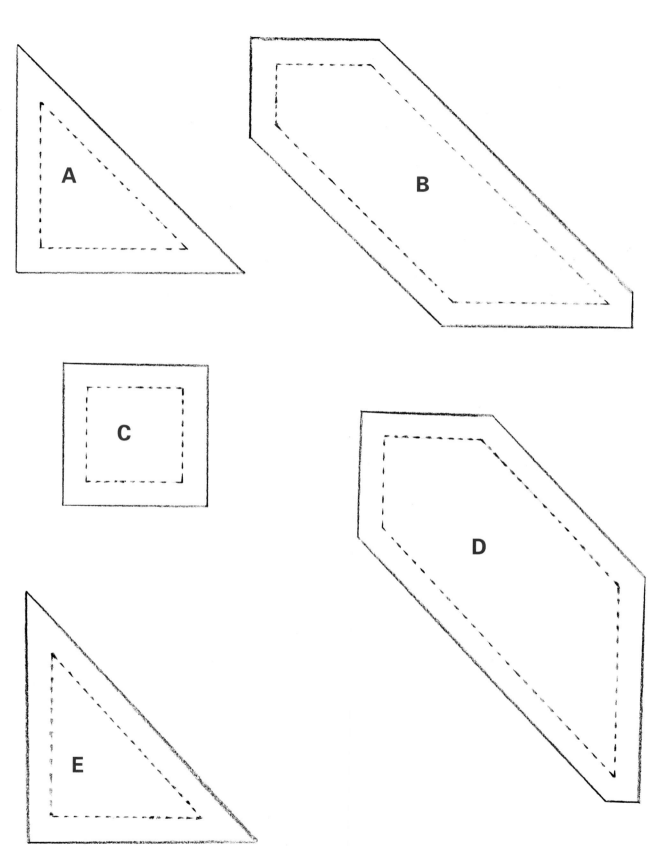

A

B

C

D

E

CHAPTER 3

Costumes and Embellishments

"Know first who you are and then adorn yourself accordingly."
—Euripedes, 480-406 BC

For thousands of years, dress has been important to perpetuate order, to preserve tradition and to express joy. This chapter pays homage to costumes and embellishments by using pieces we typically dress with to adorn home décor pieces.

Kimono Quilt

The simple and elegant kimono has no parallel in the history of costume. It has served as a sort of canvas for the Japanese artist, displaying anything from geometric patchwork to complex silk embroidery. In the imperial courts of the last millennium, ladies of nobility wore "12-layer dresses." This unique dress consisted of as many as 12 layers of undergarments, worn under a long, pleated robe. Each layer was a different color of fabric. It was so expertly designed that a line of color displaying each layer was visible at the neckline, the sleeve, and the hem. After 1500, the cultural trend was toward simplification in dress, customs, and almost all other aspects of daily life. After several decades, the layers of the dress were gradually discarded until the innermost garment became the kimono. Many centuries later, the distinctive kimono is utilitarian, yet aesthetic, serving both as a practical robe and as an art object.

FINISHED SIZE: 42" X 55" ■ SEAM ALLOWANCES: ¼"

Materials Needed

1 yard dark pink fabric

$3/4$-yard burgundy fabric

$1/3$-yard olive fabric

$1^5/8$ yards violet print fabric

$1^3/4$ yards blue print fabric

Coordinating thread

48" x 62" piece cotton quilt batting

$3^1/3$ yards cotton batting (backing)

$5^3/4$ yards $2^1/2$"-wide green print bias strip

Embroidery floss, as follows:

- 1 skein pink
- 1 skein brown
- 1 skein green

$1/4$- to $1/2$-yard each of the following fabrics (kimonos):

- moss green
- moss green print
- tan print
- light pink print
- dark pink print
- light blue print
- lavender print
- various multi-prints

Tracing paper

Air-soluble marking pen

Cutting Plan

1. With the tracing paper, make the templates for both kimonos from the originals found on pages 56 through 59. Broken lines indicate seam lines.

2. For Kimono A, cut the following:
   - 10 "A" shapes from the fabric colors of choice
   - 20 "B" shapes from the fabric colors of choice
   - 10 "C" shapes from dark pink fabric
   - 10 "D" shapes from the dark pink fabric

3. For Kimono B, cut the following:
   - 5 "A" shapes from the burgundy fabric
   - 5 reverse "A" shapes from the burgundy fabric*
   - 5 "B" shapes from the fabric colors of choice
   - 5 reverse "B" shapes from the fabric colors of choice*
   - 5 "C" shapes from the burgundy fabric
   - 5 reverse "C" shapes from the burgundy fabric*
   - 5 "D" triangles from the fabric colors of choice
   - 5 reverse "D" triangles from the fabric colors of choice*
   - 5 "E" shapes from the burgundy fabric
   - 5 reverse "E" shapes from the burgundy fabric*
   - 10 "F" shapes from the fabric colors of choice
   - 10 "G" shapes (optional) from the fabric colors of choice

4. For the assembly, cut the following:
   - 4 40" x 2" strips from the olive fabric
   - 20 2" x $4^3/4$" strips from various print fabrics (collars)
   - 2 2" x $42^1/2$" strips from the violet print fabric
   - 2 2" x 55" strips from the violet print fabric

*Reverse the templates to create mirror-image shapes.

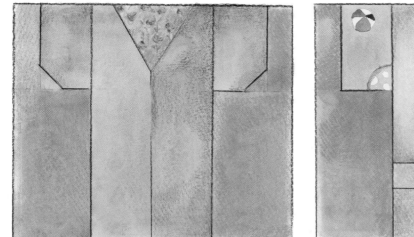

Sample Kimono A blocks.

Kimono A Quilt Blocks

The finished Kimono A quilt blocks measure 10$\frac{1}{2}$" x 9". The kimonos have wide sleeves and are set in a dark pink background. Vary the styles by changing the sleeve and the robe details. On the templates, the variations are indicated with a blue line. Refer to the sample blocks here for guidance.

1. Being sure to use the Kimono A fabric pieces, stitch shape "A" to "C," so that "A" is to the right of "C."

2. Stitch "A-C" to "D," as shown in Figure 3-1.

3. Referring to Figure 3-2, stitch the long side of the pieced rectangle to "B," so that "B" is to the right of the pieced section. Press.

4. Repeat steps 1 through 3, this time reversing "A" and "C" in step 1 so that "A" is now to the left of "C", and "B" in step 3 is now to the left of the pieced section. This results in a mirror-image piece to the first piece created. Press.

5. Stitch the two pieced sections together to complete the block. Press.

6. Repeat steps 1 through 5 nine more times to make a total of 10 Kimono A quilt blocks. (Include several with variations, if desired.)

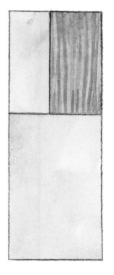

Figure 3-1

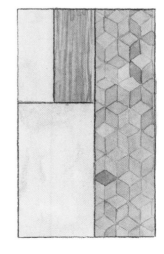

Figure 3-2

Sample Kimono B blocks, above and at right.

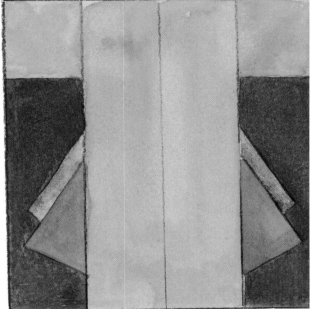

Kimono B Quilt Blocks

The finished Kimono B quilt blocks measure 9" square. The kimonos have narrow sleeves and are set in a burgundy background. Vary the style by changing the robe profile. Refer to the sample blocks for guidance. Templates "A" through "E" are for the winged profile. Substitute template "G" for "A" through "E" when making the simple profile.

1. Referring to Figure 3-3, stitch "A" to "B" and "C" to "D," making sure to use the Kimono B pieces.

2. Stitch "A-B" to "C-D" and then "E" to the pieced section, as shown in Figure 3-4.

Figure 3-3

Figure 3-4

52

3. Referring to Figure 3-5, stitch "F" to the top of the pieced rectangle. Press.

4. Stitch one of the leftover "B" fabric pieces from Kimono A to the pieced rectangle, so that "B" is to the right of the pieced section, as shown in Figure 3-6 on the facing page. Press.

5. Repeat steps 1 through 4, this time using the reverse shapes in place of the regular ones for steps 1 and 2 and stitching the "B" piece of step 4 to the right of the pieced section to create a mirror-image of the first block half. Press.

6. Stitch pieced rectangles together to complete the block.

7. Repeat steps 1 through 6 nine more times to make a total of 10 Kimono B quilt blocks. (Include several with the simple profile, if desired.)

Figure 3-5

Assembly

1. Starting with a Kimono A block, alternate the A-blocks with the B-blocks and stitch four blocks together at the sides to make a horizontal row. Press. Repeat to make a total of three rows.

2. Stitch one 40" x 2" olive strip to the bottom of one of the pieced rows. Press. Repeat with a second row.

3. Starting with a Kimono B block, alternate the B-blocks with the A-blocks and stitch four blocks together at the sides. Press. Repeat to make a second row.

4. Stitch one 40" x 2" olive strip to the bottom of one of these pieced rows. Press. Repeat for the second row.

Figure 3-6

5. Fold each 2" x 4³/₄" collar strip in half lengthwise and press.

6. With the folded edge on top, place one strip horizontally on the work surface and referring to Figure 3-7, fold the ends in. Press. Repeat for the remaining collar strips.

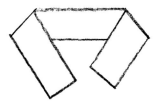

Figure 3-7

7. With the folded side up, center and stitch the collars to the tops of the robes, as shown in Figure 3-8. When the horizontal rows of the quilt top are stitched together, the collars will be pressed up on the olive strips.

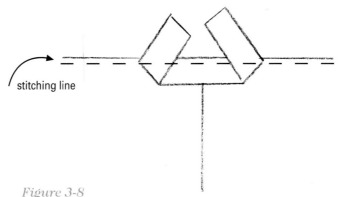

stitching line

Figure 3-8

8. Referring to Figure 3-9, note that since A-blocks are wider than B-blocks, the kimono rows will be staggered when stitched together. Beginning with an A-block in the top left corner, align the center seams of the kimonos and stitch the kimono rows together. The bottom row will have no olive strip. Press.

9. With the air-soluble marking pen, mark the stitching line on the sides of the pieced section. (The stitching line is $1/4$" from the edge of the B-blocks.) Trim the edges.

10. Starting and stopping $1/4$" from each edge, center and stitch the two 2" x $42^1/_2$" violet print strips to the top and the bottom of the quilt center. Press.

11. Stitch the two 2" x 55" violet print strips to the left and right sides of the quilt center.

12. Miter the corners, as instructed on page 7. Press.

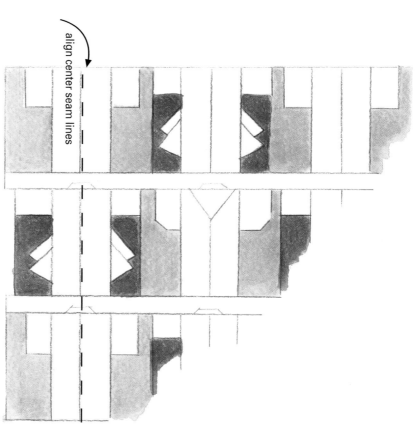

align center seam lines

Figure 3-9

Quilting

1. As an option, mark the desired quilt design with the marking pen. The machine-quilting on the photo model consists of straight lines and stippling and required no marked lines. The outlines of the kimonos and the fabric patterns served as stitching guides.

2. Piece the backing fabric together to make a 48" x 62" rectangle. Press.

3. With the wrong-side up, place the backing fabric on the work surface. Carefully smooth out any folds and center the batting on top of the backing fabric. With the right-side up, center the quilt top on the quilt batting.

4. Secure all layers with pins or with long basting stitches.

5. Machine-quilt as desired, referring to the instructions on page 7, if needed.

6. Remove the pins or the basting stitches, trim the threads, and then trim the edge of the quilt.

7. Stitch the bias binding around the edge of the quilt, referring to the binding on page 8, if necessary.

8. Using four strands of embroidery floss, stitch the diagonal stitches to the sleeves of selected kimonos, as shown in the accompanying photo at right.

Use embroidery floss to stitch the decorative detail on the sleeves.

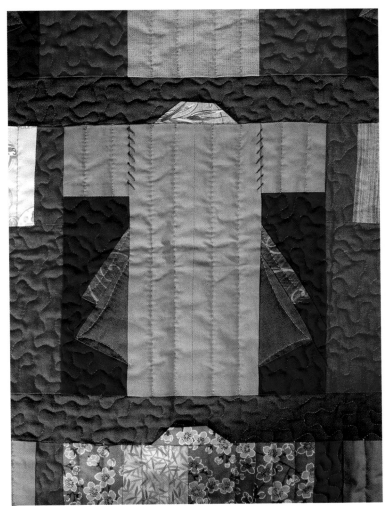

Templates

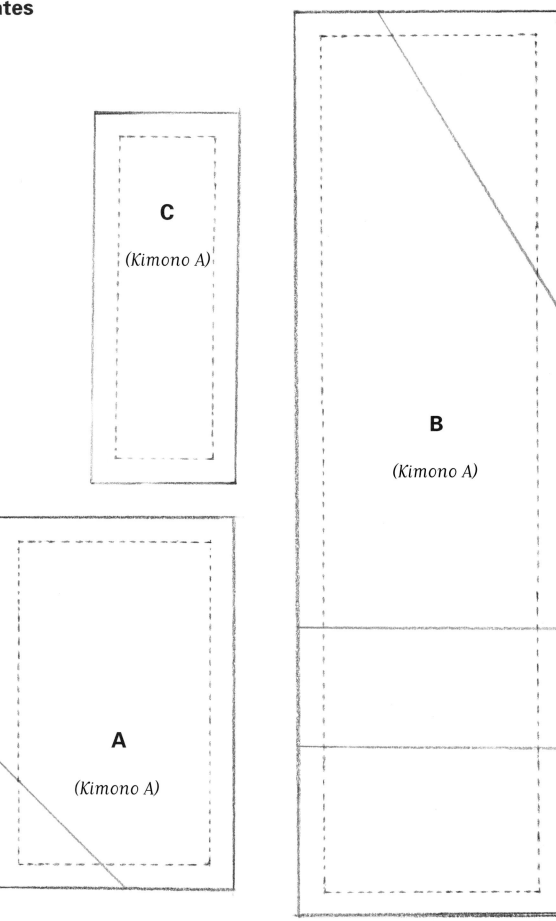

C

(Kimono A)

B

(Kimono A)

A

(Kimono A)

D

(Kimono A)

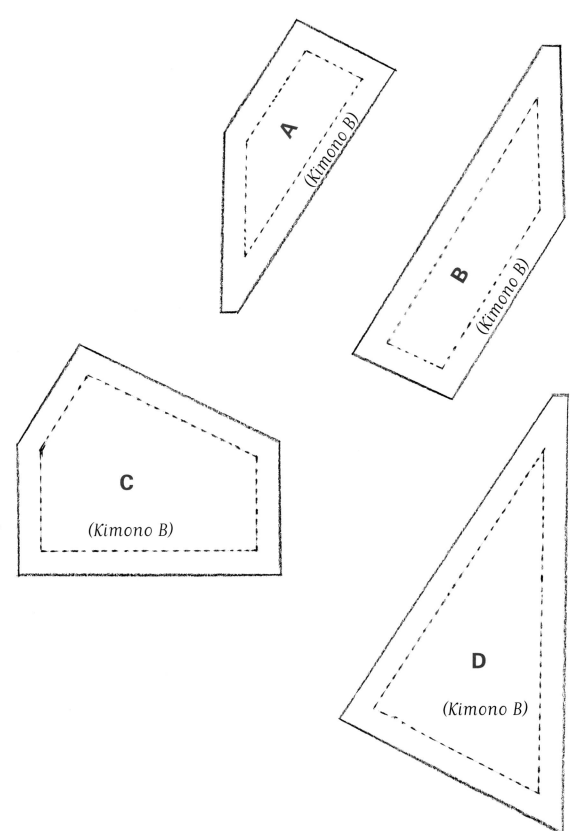

A
(Kimono B)

B
(Kimono B)

C
(Kimono B)

D
(Kimono B)

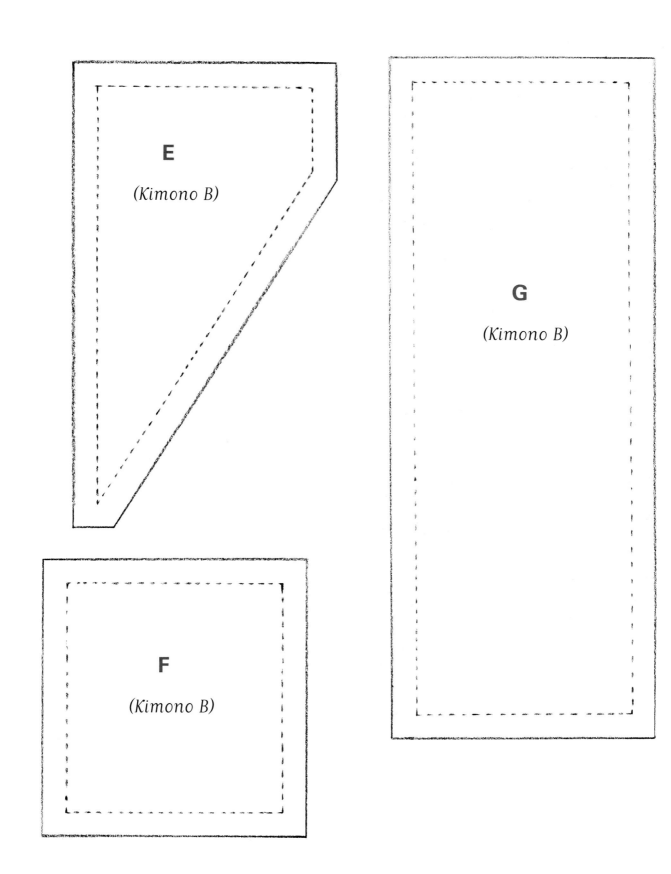

E
(Kimono B)

F
(Kimono B)

G
(Kimono B)

Kimono Quilt Templates

Fan Quilt

"Ten thousand years of life to you." This is the wish chanted by street singers on the first day of the new year. They stroll in pairs in provincial towns and cities of Japan, with one beating a drum and the other waving a fan. The fan is used in the procession because it is a symbol of life, of good luck, and of future prosperity. The expansion of the fan represents expanding fortunes and the road toward eternity. The folding fan was invented in the seventh century in a province near Kyoto. The inventor was intrigued by the mechanics of a bat wing, so he fashioned cypress bark to expand and contract in the same manner. Given as gifts, the fan delighted the early recipients who were able to fold up the fans and tuck them into their dress or shirtsleeves.

FINISHED SIZE: 42" X 45" ■ SEAM ALLOWANCES: ¼"

Materials Needed

1⅓ yards red print fabric
1⅓ yards black fabric
1⅓ yards adobe print fabric
1⅓ yards light green fabric
1⅓ yards medium green print fabric
1⅓ yards dark blue print fabric
1⅓ yards dark brown print fabric
¼-yard each of the following fabrics (fans):
- light green print
- peach print
- cream print
- blue metallic weave gold
- burnt orange print
- dark brown print
- gray print

7mm silk ribbon, as follows:
- 1 skein lavender
- 1 skein olive
- 1 skein orange

Matching threads for hand-appliqué (fans)
Matching threads for machine-stitching (ribbons)
Contrasting threads for machine-appliqué (sticks)
Tracing paper
Air-soluble marking pen
1 yard lightweight non-woven stabilizer for machine embroidery
44" x 47" piece cotton quilt batting
1½ yards cotton fabric (backing)
5 yards ½"-wide black bias binding

Cutting Plan

1. With the tracing paper, make the templates from the originals found on pages 66 and 67. Broken lines indicate seam lines.

2. Cut the following, noting any referenced steps first, before cutting:
   - 3 $8\frac{1}{8}$" x $45\frac{1}{2}$" strips from the red print fabric
   - 21 fan shapes from selected fabrics, adding ¼" around the edge of each template (note Appliqué step 1 instructions)
   - 6 half-fan shapes from selected fabrics, adding ¼" around the edge of each template (note Appliqué step 1 instructions)
   - 21 4" squares from the stabilizer
   - $3\frac{1}{2}$" x $45\frac{1}{2}$" strip from the adobe print fabric
   - 3 $1\frac{1}{4}$" x $45\frac{1}{2}$" strips from the black fabric
   - 2" x $45\frac{1}{2}$" strip from the light green fabric
   - 2" x $45\frac{1}{2}$" strip from the dark blue print fabric
   - $3\frac{1}{2}$" x $45\frac{1}{2}$" strip from the medium green fabric
   - 2 4" x $45\frac{1}{2}$" strips from the dark brown print fabric

Appliqué

1. On the right sides of the selected fan fabrics, mark 21 fan shapes with the air-soluble marking pen. Allow at least $1/2$" between shapes to turn the edges under for appliqué, as detailed in the Needle-Turned Appliqué instructions on page 9. Note that six fans are cropped and only the right or the left half of the fan shape is required.

2. With the right-side up, place one $8^1/8$" x $45^1/2$" red strip on the work surface. This strip will be the center strip in the assembled quilt top.

3. Referring to Figure 3-10, pin fans #3, #6, and #8 in place and using matching thread colors, hand-appliqué the fans to the strip.

4. Place the appliquéd strip on the work surface and noting the overlaps, pin the remaining fans in place. Hand-appliqué the fans to the strip.

5. Noting that the fans are placed 2" lower on the side strips, as shown in the accompanying photo below, repeat steps 2 through 3 with remaining red strips.

6. With the marking pen, mark the fan sticks coming from the bottom of each fan, as shown in the photo on the next page.

7. Pin one 4" stabilizer square to the wrong side of one red strip, behind one set of marked sticks.

8. On a scrap of fabric, satin stitch a short straight line by machine. Adjust your machine to the desired line width and coverage. The width of the sticks on the photo model are slightly wider than $1/16$".

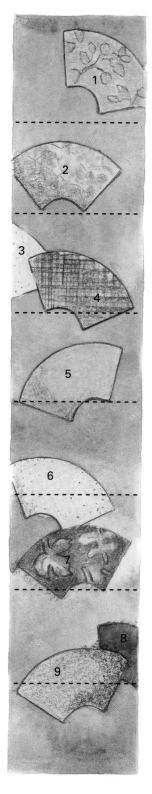

Figure 3-10

The fan placement on the side strips begins 2" lower than that on the center strip.

9. With contrasting thread, machine-stitch the sticks beneath one fan. Trim the thread ends.

10. Trim the stabilizer, as shown in Figure 3-11 below.

11. Using a variety of contrasting thread colors, repeat steps 7 through 9 for the remaining sticks.

Assembly

1. Stitch the $3^1/_2$" x $45^1/_2$" adobe print strip to the left side of the left fan strip. Press.

2. Stitch together the long sides of one $1^1/_4$" x $45^1/_2$" black strip and the 2" x $45^1/_2$" light green strip. Press.

3. Stitch the long side of the black-light green strip to the left side of the center fan strip, with the light green portion closest to the fan strip. Press.

4. Repeat step 2 with the other $1^1/_4$" x $45^1/_2$" black strips and the 2" x $45^1/_2$" dark blue print strip.

5. Stitch the long side of the black-blue print strip to the left side of the right fan strip, with the blue portion closest to the fan strip. Press.

6. Repeat step 2 with last $1^1/_4$" x $45^1/_2$" black strip and $3^1/_2$" x $45^1/_2$" medium green strip.

7. Stitch the long side of the black-medium green strip to the right side of the right fan strip, with the black portion closest to the fan strip. Press.

8. Stitch the long sides of the side sections to the center section. Press.

9. Stitch the 4" x $45^1/_2$" dark brown strips to the right and the left sides of the quilt center. Press.

Figure 3-11

Note the placement of the fan sticks, shown above.

Did You Know?

It is difficult to find a historical object with a greater variety of uses than the fan. In Asian cultures, the fan has been used as a bellow to fan flames, as a winnowing tool to separate chaff from grain, as an album on which to write and exchange sentiments, and as a defensive weapon in battle. The most charming use of the fan, however, is when friends or lovers exchange it at parting. The possession of the fan during absence is thought to ensure a happy reunion.

Machine-quilt along the seam lines, around the fans and sticks, and in a free-form zigzag inside various fans.

Quilting

1. As an option, mark the desired quilt design with the marking pen. The photo model is machine-quilted along the seam lines, around the fans, and around the sticks. Selected fan centers are machine-quilted in a horizontal zigzag pattern, as shown above. Since the seams and the fans served as stitching guides, and the zigzag lines are free-form, the photo model required no marked lines.

2. With the wrong-side up, place the backing fabric on the work surface. Carefully smooth out any folds and center the batting on top of the backing fabric. With the right side up, center the quilt top on the quilt batting.

3. Secure all layers with pins or with long basting stitches.

4. Machine-quilt as desired, referring to the instructions on page 7, if needed.

5. Remove the pins or the basting stitches and trim the thread ends.

6. With the air-soluble marking pen, draw the lines on the selected fans for ribbon placement, as indicated in the photo at right.

7. Cut the ribbon into 4$\frac{1}{2}$" lengths.

8. With matching thread, machine-stitch the ribbon on the marked lines. Trim the ribbon ends.

Note the ribbon placement.

9. Trim the edge of the quilt and then stitch the bias binding around the edge, referring to the binding instructions on page 8, if necessary.

Fan

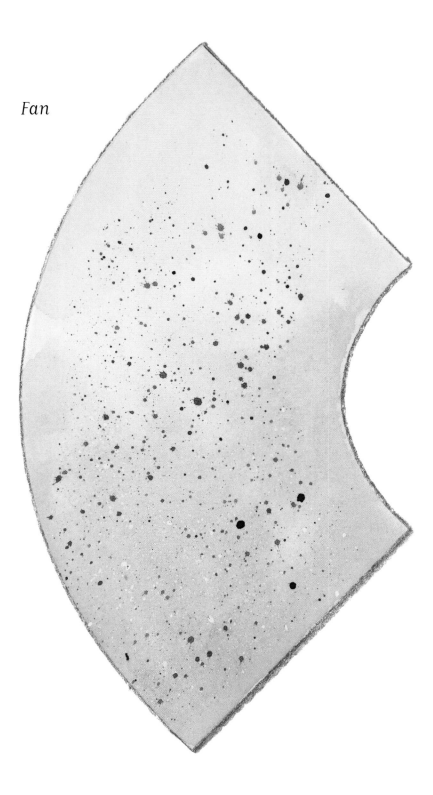

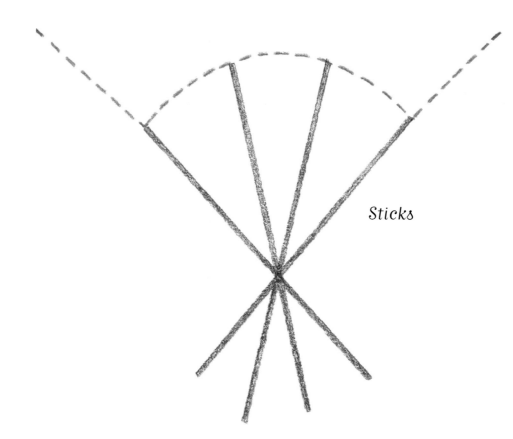

Sticks

Sunflower Pillow

This pillow design was inspired by an arrangement of overlapping flowers placed strategically in the bottom corner of an antique kimono.

FINISHED SIZE: 13" SQUARE ■ SEAM ALLOWANCES: ¹/₄"

Materials Needed

½-yard maize cotton fabric

⅛-yard olive print fabric

Matching threads for hand-appliqué

Gold thread

Tracing paper

Air-soluble marking pen

14" square muslin

14" square cotton quilt batting

13½" square cotton fabric (pillow back)

13" pillow form

1½ yards 6.4mm gold cord

1½ yards 6.4mm gold cord

Scraps of cotton fabric in the following colors (appliqué):

- white
- dark red
- red print
- yellow print
- gold print
- peach
- peach print
- blue
- green print
- light brown print

Cutting Plan

1. With the tracing paper, make the templates from the originals found on pages 73 and 74. Broken lines indicate seam lines.

2. Cut the following, noting any referenced steps first, before cutting:
   - 2½" x 13½" strip from the olive print fabric
   - 2" x 13½" strip from the maize fabric
   - 10" x 13½" rectangle from the maize fabric
   - 1 set Arc A pieces from selected fabrics, adding ¼" around the edge of each template (note Appliqué step 2 instructions)
   - 1 set Arc B pieces from selected fabrics, adding ¼" around the edge of each template (note Appliqué step 2 instructions)
   - 1 set Arc C pieces from selected fabrics, adding ¼" around the edge of each template (note Appliqué step 2 instructions)

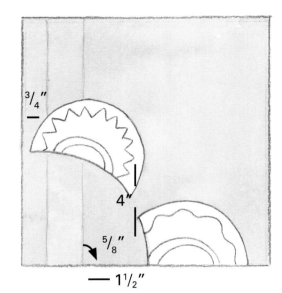

Figure 3-14   *Figure 3-15*

Appliqué

1. With long sides together, stitch the $2\frac{1}{2}$" x $13\frac{1}{2}$" olive strip between the 2" x $13\frac{1}{2}$" maize strip and the 10" x $13\frac{1}{2}$" maize rectangle to create a square. Press.

2. On the right sides of the selected Arc A fabrics, mark the shapes with the air-soluble marking pen. Allow at least $\frac{1}{4}$" around each shape to turn the edges under for appliqué, as detailed in the Needle-Turned Appliqué instructions on page 9.

3. Referring to Figure 3-14 for placement, pin and hand-appliqué the Arc A pieces to the maize-olive square in the following sequence: background arc, petals, rim, and center.

4. Repeat step 2 with the Arc B templates.

5. Referring to Figure 3-15 for placement, pin and hand-appliqué the Arc B pieces to the background in the following sequence: background arc, petals, rim, and center.

6. Repeat step 2 with the Arc C templates.

7. Referring to Figure 3-16 for placement, pin and hand-appliqué the Arc C pieces to the background in the following sequence: large background arc, small background arc, petals, and center.

Figure 3-16 *Figure 3-17*

Quilting

1. With the marking pen, mark the vertical lines for quilting, as indicated in Figure 3-17.

2. Place the muslin on the work surface. Place the batting on the muslin. With the right-side up, center the pillow top on the quilt batting.

3. Secure all layers with pins or with basting stitches.

4. Machine-quilt along the marked lines and around the appliquéd shapes. Trim the edges.

Pillow Assembly

1. With the right sides together, pin the pillow front to the pillow back and stitch together, leaving an 8" opening on one side. Trim the excess fabric at the corners.

2. Turn right-side out, press, and insert the pillow form.

3. Whipstitch the opening closed.

4. Starting at the center bottom, hand-stitch the wide cord to the pillow at the seam. Stitch around the entire pillow and abut the cord ends together.

5. From the narrow cord, cut one 12", one 14", and one 18" length.

Place the short lengths on the work surface.

Place the looped cord behind the shorter lengths of cord.

Pull the ends through to make a knot.

6. Place the short lengths on the work surface, as shown above left.

7. Fold the 18" piece in half lengthwise to form a loop and place the loop behind the short lengths, as shown above center.

8. Insert the ends around the short lengths and through the loop to form a knot, as shown above right. Tie a knot at the end of each length and trim the excess cord.

9. Hand-stitch the knot to the pillow to cover the ends of the wide cord.

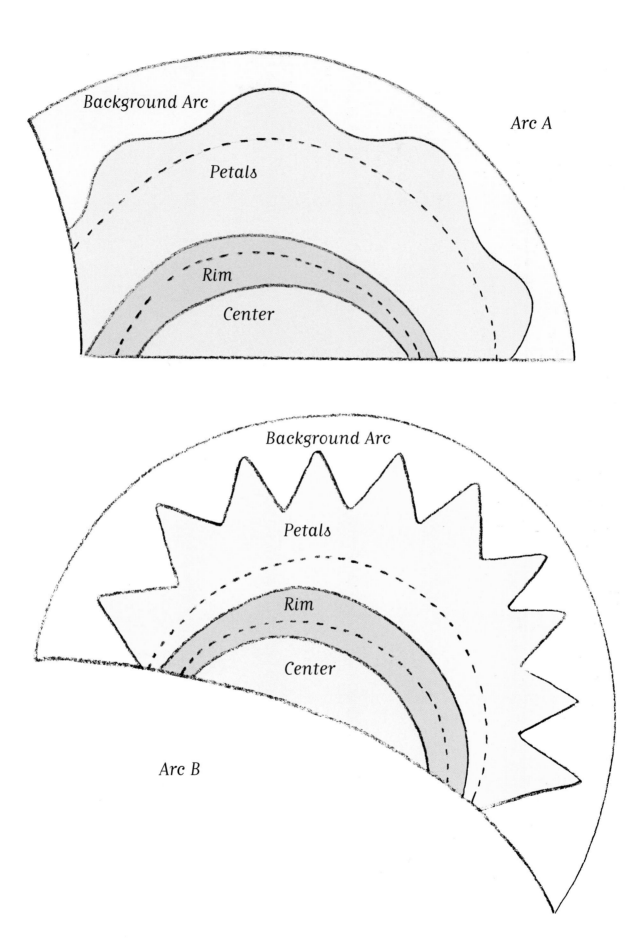

Background Arc

Arc A

Petals

Rim

Center

Background Arc

Petals

Rim

Center

Arc B

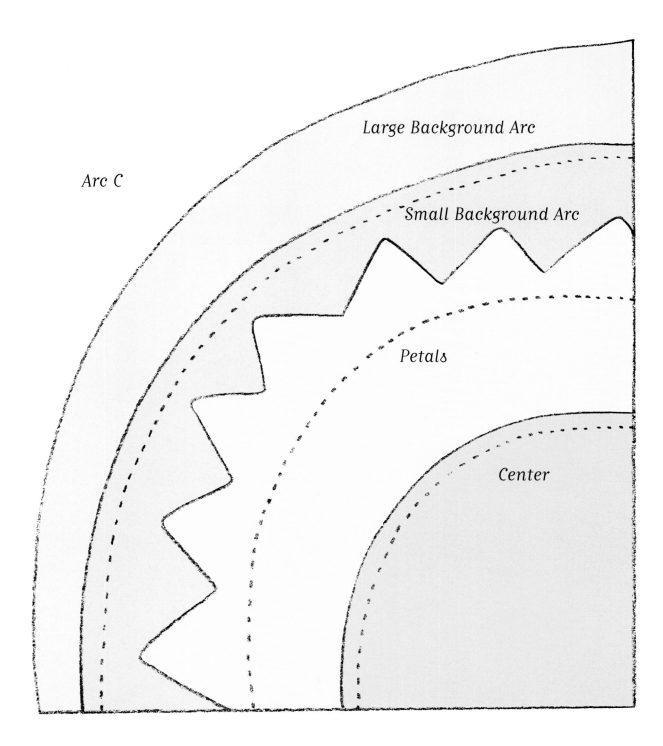

Large Background Arc

Arc C

Small Background Arc

Petals

Center

Cloud Medallion Pillow

Medallions, such as this stylized cloud, are appliquéd or stamped onto elaborate theater costumes.

FINISHED SIZE: 13" SQUARE ■ SEAM ALLOWANCES: ¹/₄"

Materials Needed

¹/₂-yard maize cotton fabric	Air-soluble marking pen
¹/₄-yard blue fabric	14" square muslin
Scraps of cotton fabric in a variety of	14" square cotton quilt batting
coordinating colors and prints (hexagons)	13¹/₂" square cotton fabric for pillow back
Blue thread	13" pillow form
Gold thread	1¹/₂ yards 6.4mm gold cord
Tracing paper	1¹/₂ yards 6.4mm gold cord

Cutting Plan

1. With the tracing paper, make the templates from the originals found on page 79. Broken lines indicate seam lines.

2. Cut the following, noting any referenced steps first, before cutting:
   - 13¹/₂" x 13¹/₂" square from the maize fabric
   - 32 hexagon shapes from selected fabric scraps, adding ¹/₄" around the edge of each template (note Appliqué step 1 instructions)
   - 1 set of cloud pieces from the blue fabric, adding ¹/₄" around the edge of each template piece (note Appliqué step 5 instructions)

Appliqué

1. On the wrong-side of one fabric scrap, draw a hexagon with the air-soluble marking pen. Allow at least ¹/₄" around each seam allowance, and to turn the edges under for appliqué, as detailed in the Needle-Turned Appliqué instructions on page 9. Continue making hexagon pieces until you have 32 total.

2. Matching the marked lines, hand-stitch the hexagons together, as shown in Figure 3-18, to make two "A" configurations. Press.

Figure 3-18

3. Matching the marked lines, hand-stitch the hexagons together, as shown in Figure 3-19, to make two "B" configurations. Press.

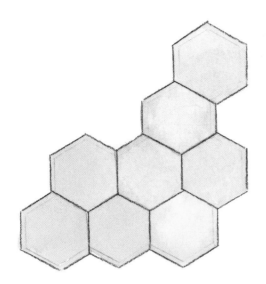

Figure 3-19

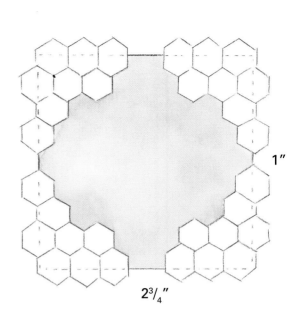

1"

2³/₄"

Figure 3-20

4. Referring to Figure 3-20 for placement, pin the hexagon sections to the corners of the square. Turn the edges under and hand-appliqué the inside edges of the hexagon sections to the square. The bottom and outside edges of the hexagon sections will overlap the maize square.

5. On the blue fabric, draw the shapes with the air-soluble marking pen. Allow at least ¼" around each shape to turn the edges under for appliqué, referring to the Needle-Turned Appliqué instructions on page 9, if needed.

6. Center and pin the cloud pieces to the maize square. Hand-appliqué the shapes to the square, as shown below.

Center and hand-applique the cloud shape to the center of the maize square.

Quilting

1. Place the muslin on the work surface. Place the batting on the muslin. With the right-side up, center the pillow top on the quilt batting.

2. Secure all layers with pins or with basting stitches.

3. Machine-quilt around the cloud shapes and trim the edges.

Pillow Assembly

1. With the right sides together, pin the pillow front to the pillow back and stitch together, leaving an 8" opening on one side. Trim the excess fabric at the corners.

2. Turn right-side out, press, and insert the pillow form.

3. Whipstitch the opening closed.

4. Starting at the center bottom, hand-stitch the wide cord to the pillow at the seam. Stitch around the entire pillow and abut the cord ends together.

5. From the narrow cord, cut one 12", one 14", and one 18" length.

6. Place the short lengths on the work surface, as shown below left.

7. Fold the 18" piece in half lengthwise to form a loop and place the loop behind the short lengths, as shown below center.

8. Insert the ends around the short lengths and through the loop to form a knot, as shown below right. Tie a knot at the end of each length and trim the excess cord.

9. Hand-stitch the knot to the pillow to cover the ends of the wide cord.

Place the short lengths on the work surface.

Place the looped cord behind the shorter lengths of cord.

Pull the ends through to make a knot.

Hexagon

Cloud

No Mask Table Runner

In ancient times, farmers performed pantomime dances in their fields to request blessings from the deity. Music and masks were added, and the dances became more sophisticated. They were performed in temples and in palaces and were often both dramatic and comical. The most noteworthy, the "No" plays, were written in the fourteenth and fifteenth centuries with "No" meaning performance. These refined masks became an integral part of the performance.

FINISHED SIZE: 14" X 40" ■ SEAM ALLOWANCE: ¹⁄₄"

Materials Needed

1 yard floral cotton fabric

$\frac{1}{3}$-yard rust print cotton fabric

$\frac{1}{4}$-yard ivory print cotton fabric

Matching thread for appliqué

Coordinating thread for assembly

Scraps of geometric print cotton fabric

Black thread

Red thread

Tracing paper

Air-soluble marking pen

Pink crayon

Cutting Plan

1. With the tracing paper, make the templates from the originals found on page 83. Broken lines indicate seam lines.

2. Cut the following, noting any referenced steps first, before cutting:
   - $14\frac{1}{2}$" x $11\frac{1}{2}$" rectangle from the rust print fabric
   - 1 face piece from the ivory print fabric, adding $\frac{1}{4}$" around the edge of the template (note Appliqué step 1 instructions)
   - 2 $2\frac{1}{4}$"-diameter circles from the geometric print fabric, adding $\frac{1}{8}$" around the edge
   - $1\frac{3}{4}$"-diameter circle from the geometric print fabric, adding $\frac{1}{8}$" around the edge
   - $14\frac{1}{2}$" x $4\frac{1}{2}$" rectangle from the floral fabric
   - $14\frac{1}{2}$" x 26" rectangle from the floral fabric
   - $14\frac{1}{2}$" x $40\frac{1}{2}$" rectangle from the floral fabric

Appliqué

1. On the right-side of the ivory print fabric, draw the face with the air-soluble marking pen. Mark the hairline and the face. Referring to the Needle-Turned Appliqué instructions on page 9, allow $\frac{1}{4}$" around the marked line.

2. With the short sides of the rust print rectangle vertical, center and pin the ivory face on the rectangle and hand-appliqué the face in place.

3. Adjust the machine to the widest available satin stitch. On a scrap of fabric, satin stitch a short, straight line by machine. Adjust the coverage.

4. With the black thread, satin stitch along the marked hairline on the face and along the appliquéd edge. Fill in stitched rows to create two solid areas of hair.

5. Adjust the machine to a narrow satin stitch ($1/32$" wide). Satin stitch the top and bottom eyelids and pupils.

6. Adjust the machine to a medium satin stitch ($1/16$" wide). Satin stitch the nostrils and center lip line in black and then switch to red thread to satin stitch the top and bottom lip, as shown at right.

7. Pin the geometric print circles to the rust print rectangle, as shown below, and hand-appliqué the circles to the rectangle.

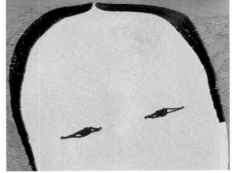

Use black thread to satin stitch the hair and eyes onto the face.

Complete the Table Runner

1. Stitch the $14 1/2$" x $4 1/2$" floral rectangle to the bottom of the rust appliquéd rectangle and the $14 1/2$" x 26" floral rectangle to the top. Press.

2. With the right sides together, stitch the front of the table runner to the $14 1/2$" x $40 1/2$" floral rectangle back, leaving a 5″ opening along one side. Trim the excess fabric from the corners.

3. Turn right-side out and press.

4. Whipstitch the opening closed.

5. With the pink crayon, highlight the forehead and the chin. Areas for highlight are indicated on the template piece with a broken line.

Use a black satin stitch on the nostrils and center lip line and red on the top and bottom lips.

Position the geometric print circles on the rust rectangle and hand-appliqué in place.

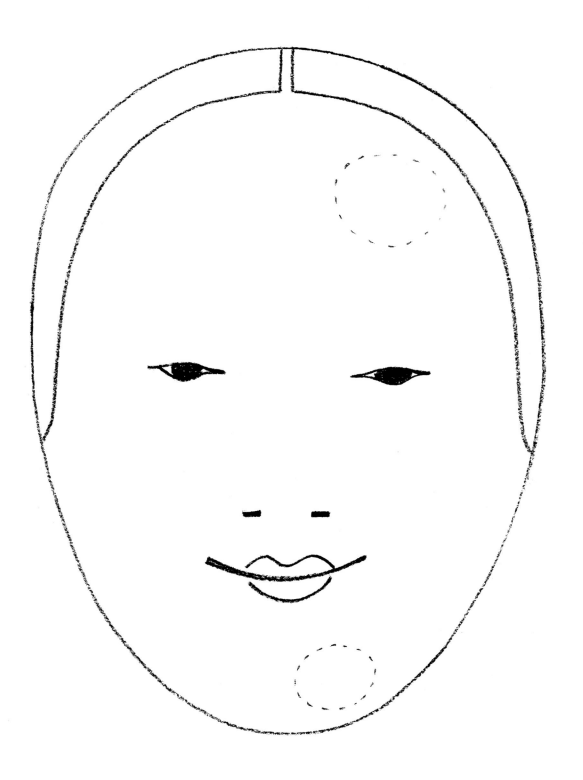

CHAPTER 4

Water

Water, earth, wood,

fire, and metal:

The five basic elements that

hold a prominent place in Japanese

cultural and legendary tradition.

Water is a magical, moving, living

part of the universe. Adding

a single drop of pigment can

transform it into liquid wizardry.

Koi Watercolor Wall Hanging

A sampler of dissimilar patterns achieves visual unity by using one color palette of soft watercolor pastels. Although each section is distinctly different in pattern and scale, (no pun intended), the subtle color scheme allows the eye to float around the surface of the quilt smoothly with all of the elements connected. Then a pair of fish is stirred into the mix to add asymmetrical interest. Graceful lines of swimming koi are the perfect complement to the surrounding arrangement of rigid geometric patterns. According to experts, ornamental koi fish originated in Persia and were exported to China and Japan. The Japanese word for koi—"nishikigo"—means brocaded carp. Today these high-class carp are bred for color, color pattern, body shape, and fin shape. Most often sporting bright colors of white, orange, blue, or black, the fabric fish here are rendered in soft colors to blend into the larger composition.

FINISHED SIZE: 38" X 43" ■ SEAM ALLOWANCES: ¹/₄"

Materials Needed

³/₄-yard wheat silk fabric

¹/₃-yard lavender cotton fabric

¹/₈-yard lavender silk fabric

¹/₈-yard lavender print cotton fabric

¹/₈-yard sage green pinstripe silk fabric

¹/₄-yard light green satin fabric

¹/₂-yard light blue print cotton fabric

¹/₂-yard medium blue print cotton fabric

¹/₄-yard pink moiré fabric

¹/₄-yard purple cotton fabric

¹/₄-yard tan print fabric

¹/₄-yard cream print cotton fabric

¹/₄-yard ivory print cotton fabric

1³/₄ yards cream cotton fabric

Gray thread

Cream thread

Scraps of the following cotton fabrics (appliqué):
- pink print
- brown print
- periwinkle print
- turquoise print
- lavender print
- medium blue print

Scraps of the following cotton fabrics (harlequin pattern):
- tan
- blue

Tracing paper

Air-soluble marking pen

40" x 45" piece cotton quilt batting

1³/₄ yards cotton fabric (backing)

1³/₄ yards cotton fabric (facing)

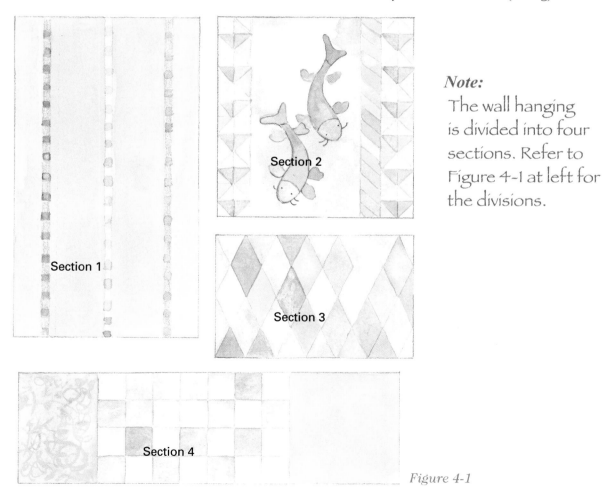

Section 1

Section 2

Section 3

Section 4

Note:
The wall hanging is divided into four sections. Refer to Figure 4-1 at left for the divisions.

Figure 4-1

Cutting Plan

1. With the tracing paper, make the templates from the originals found on pages 94 and 95. Broken lines indicate seam lines.

2. Cut the following, noting any referenced steps first, before cutting:
   - 4 $1\frac{3}{8}$" x 15" strips from the purple fabric
   - 24 triangles from the purple fabric
   - 4 $1\frac{3}{8}$" x 15" strips from the pink moiré
   - 5 diamonds from pink moiré fabric
   - 2 $1\frac{3}{8}$" x 15" strips from the ivory print fabric
   - 2 $1\frac{3}{8}$" x 15" strips from the green satin
   - 24 triangles from the green satin
   - 2 diamonds from the green satin
   - 2 3" x 27" strips from the wheat silk
   - $4\frac{1}{2}$" x 27" strip from the wheat silk
   - 3" x 27" strip from the wheat silk
   - $9\frac{1}{2}$" square from the wheat silk
   - $9\frac{1}{4}$" x 17" rectangle from the lavender fabric
   - 8 $1\frac{3}{8}$" x 4" strips from the blue fabric
   - 8 diamonds from the blue fabric
   - 5 $1\frac{3}{8}$" x 4" from the lavender print fabric
   - 4 $1\frac{3}{8}$" x 4" strips from the lavender silk
   - 24 triangles from the light blue fabric
   - 2 $2\frac{3}{4}$" x 20" strips from the light blue fabric
   - 24 triangles from the medium blue print fabric
   - 9 diamonds from the medium blue print fabric
   - 2 3" x 21" strips from the medium blue print fabric
   - 48 triangles from the ivory print fabric
   - 48 triangles from the cream print fabric
   - 2 4" x 40" strips from the cream print fabric
   - 2 4" x 45" strips from the cream print fabric
   - 1 set top fish pieces from selected fabrics
     (note Section 2 step 1)
   - 1 set bottom fish pieces from selected fabrics
     (note Section 2 step 1)
   - 4 diamonds from the tan print fabric
   - 7" x $9\frac{1}{2}$" rectangle from the tan print fabric
   - 4 diamonds from the green pinstripe silk
   - 2 4" x 40" strips from the facing fabric
   - 2 4" x 45" strips from the facing fabric

2"　　　4"　　　4"　　　2"

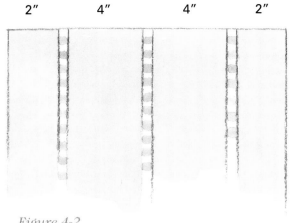

Figure 4-2

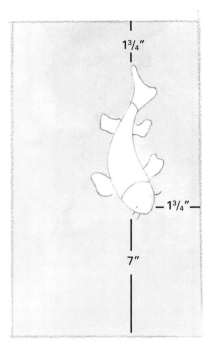

Figure 4-3

Section 1

1. Alternating two purple 1⅜" x 15" strips with two pink moiré strips of the same size, stitch the long sides together. Press.

2. Perpendicular to the seams of the purple-pink piece, cut nine 1⅜"-wide strips.

3. Stitch the short ends together to make one long strip.

4. Repeat steps 1 through 3 to make a second purple-pink strip.

5. Repeat steps 1 through 3, this time using two 1⅜" x 15" ivory satin strips with the green satin strips of the same size. (Measurements allow for seam allowance.)

6. Stitch two 3" x 27" wheat silk strips to the purple-pink and ivory-green pieced strips, as shown in Figure 4-2 above. Press.

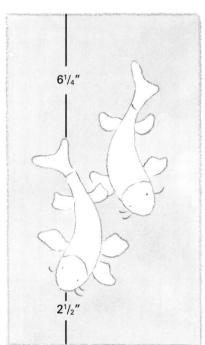

Figure 4-4

Section 2

1. On the right-side of the selected top fish fabrics, mark the shapes with the air-soluble marking pen, before cutting. Allow at least ¼" around each shape to turn the edges under for appliqué, referring to the Needle-Turned Appliqué instructions on page 9, if necessary.

2. Pin the top fish pieces in place, as indicated in Figure 4-3, and hand-appliqué them to the 9¼" x 17" lavender rectangle background in the following sequence: small double-fin shape, large double-fin shape, body, head, and tail.

3. Repeat step 1 for the bottom fish pieces.

4. Pin the bottom fish pieces in place, as shown in Figure 4-4 on the lower right of the previous page, and hand-appliqué them to the lavender background in the following sequence: double-fin shape, triple-fin shape, body, head, and tail.

5. Draw the fish eyes and whiskers with the marking pen.

6. On a scrap of fabric, satin stitch a short, straight line by machine. Adjust your machine to the desired line width and coverage. The width of the eyes and the whiskers on the photo model is slightly narrower than $1/16$".

7. With the gray thread, machine-stitch the eyes and whiskers.

8. Referring to Figure 4-5 below for sequence and angle, stagger the eight $1\frac{3}{8}$" x 4" blue strips, the five $1\frac{3}{8}$" x 4" lavender print strips, and the four $1\frac{3}{8}$" x 4" lavender silk strips, and stitch them together. Press.

9. With the air-soluble marking pen, on the wrong side of the pieced strip, draw a $1\frac{3}{4}$" x 17" rectangle. Stitch the pieced strip to the left side of the appliquéd rectangle. Press.

Hand-appliqué the shapes to the background.

Figure 4-5

10. Stitch one purple, one light blue, one green satin, one medium blue print, and four ivory print triangles together to make a square, as shown in Figure 4-6. Press. Repeat to make a total of six squares.

11. Replace the ivory print triangles used in step 10 with cream print triangles.

12. Alternating squares from step 10 and 11, stitch six together to make a vertical strip. Press. Repeat to make a second vertical strip. Stitch the vertical strips to the sides of the appliquéd triangle.

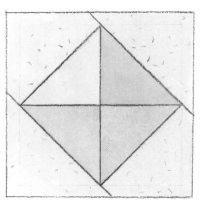

Figure 4-6

Section 3

1. Stitch together the 32 diamond shapes in a random pattern. Press.

2. On the wrong-side of this pieced section, mark a 16" x 10" rectangle.

Section 4

1. Alternating each of the two $2^3/_4$" x 20" light blue strips with the two 3" x 21" blue print strips, stitch the long sides together.

2. Perpendicular to the seams, cut seven $2^3/_4$" x $9^1/_2$" strips.

3. Rotating every other strip, stitch them together to make a checkerboard pattern. Press.

4. Stitch the long side of the 7" x $9^1/_2$" tan print rectangle to the left side of the pieced checkerboard.

5. Stitch the $9^1/_2$" wheat silk square to the right-side of the pieced checkerboard. Press.

Assembly

1. Stitch the four sections together, referring to the main project photo for placement.

2. Starting and stopping $1/_4$" from each edge, stitch the 4" x 40" cream strips to the top and the bottom of the quilt center, and the long 4" x 45" cream strips to the sides of the quilt center.

3. Miter the corners, as instructed on page 7. Press.

Quilting

1. Trim the backing fabric to 40" x 45". Press.

2. With the wrong-side up, place the backing fabric on the work surface. Carefully smooth out any folds and center the batting on the top of the backing fabric. With the right-side up, center the quilt top on the quilt batting.

3. Secure all layers with pins or with basting stitches.

4. Machine-quilt as desired, referring to page 7 for detailed instructions, if necessary. The project model is quilted along the seam lines and around the fish.

5. Remove the pins or the basting stitches, trim the thread ends, and trim the edge of the quilt.

6. Hem one long side of each of the four facing fabric strips.

7. Stitch the facing strips to the quilt to face the piece, referring to the Facing instructions on page 8, if needed.

Did You Know?
Koi fish are an essential accent for freshwater ponds and are often described with poetic metaphors such as living jewels and swimming flowers.

Stitch together the diamond shapes.

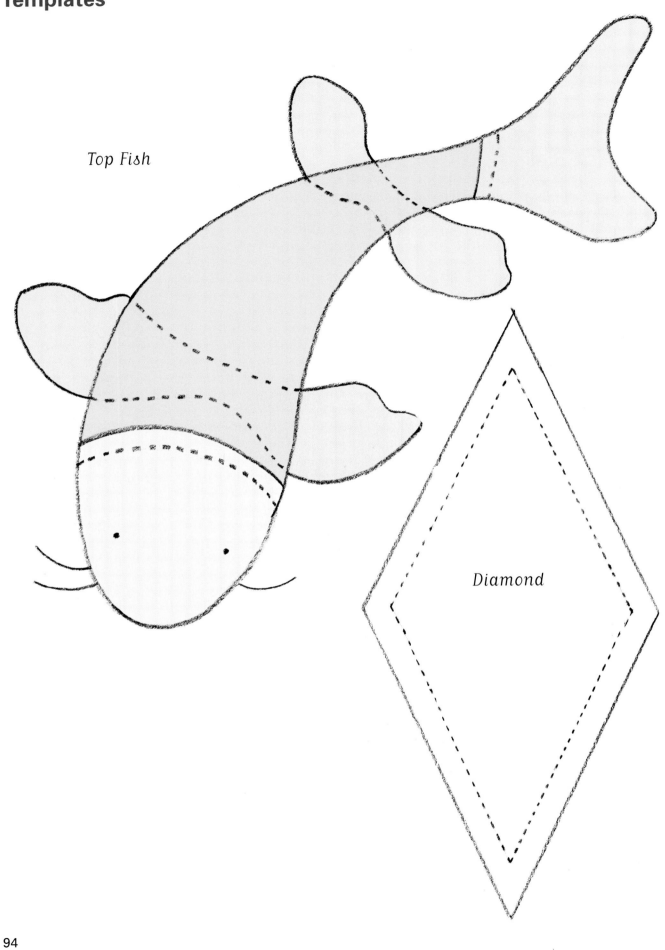

Top Fish

Diamond

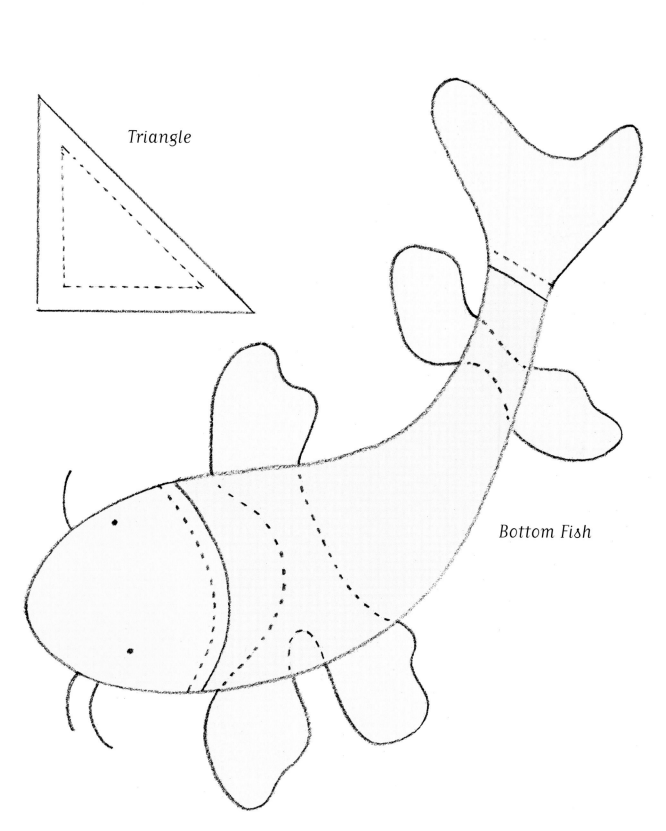

Triangle

Bottom Fish

Striped Watercolor Pillow

Designed as companions to the Koi Watercolor Wall Hanging, this pillow and the ones that follow are similar in style and color, but each has a unique asymmetrical pattern. The spaces and shapes are different, but are balanced according to visual weight and placement. The stripes of this pillow express the uniform lines that are drawn in the sand of a Zen garden.

FINISHED SIZE: 12" SQUARE ■ SEAM ALLOWANCES: ¼"

Materials Needed

$\frac{1}{4}$-yard green silk fabric

$\frac{1}{4}$-yard pink moiré fabric

$\frac{1}{4}$-yard gold moiré fabric

Scraps of the following fabric:
- cream print cotton
- gray cotton
- wheat silk

Coordinating thread

Tracing paper

Air-soluble marking pen

13" square cotton fabric (pillow back)

12" pillow form

Cutting Plan

1. With the tracing paper, make the templates from the originals found on page 99. Broken lines indicate seam lines.

2. Cut the following:
   - 6 $1\frac{3}{8}$" x $12\frac{3}{4}$" strips from the green silk fabric
   - 6 $1\frac{3}{8}$" x $12\frac{1}{4}$" strips from the pink moiré fabric
   - "A" triangle from the cream cotton fabric
   - "B" triangle from the gold moiré fabric
   - $4\frac{1}{2}$" x $2\frac{1}{2}$" rectangle from the gray cotton fabric
   - $8\frac{1}{2}$" x $2\frac{1}{2}$" rectangle from the wheat silk fabric

Assembly

1. Alternating each $1\frac{3}{8}$" x $12\frac{3}{4}$" green silk strip with the pink moiré strips of the same size, stitch the long sides of the strips together. Press.

2. Referring to Figure 4-7, use the air-soluble marking pen to mark the wrong-side of the pieced section. Trim $\frac{1}{4}$" from the marked edge.

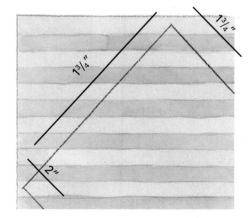

Figure 4-7

3. Rotate the pieced section, as shown in Figure 4-8.

4. Stitch the long side of the cream "A" triangle to the top left edge of the pieced stripes.

5. Stitch the long side of the gold moiré "B" triangle to the bottom left edge of the pieced stripes. Press.

6. Stitch together the short ends of the gray and wheat silk rectangles.

7. Matching the seam of the stitched rectangles to the point of the pieced stripes, stitch the sections together to complete the square. Press.

Figure 4-8

Pillow Assembly

1. With the right sides together, pin the pillow front to the pillow back and stitch together, leaving a 7" opening on one side. Trim the excess fabric from the corners.

2. Turn right-side out, press, and insert the pillow form.

3. Whipstitch the opening closed.

Stitched pillow front should look like this.

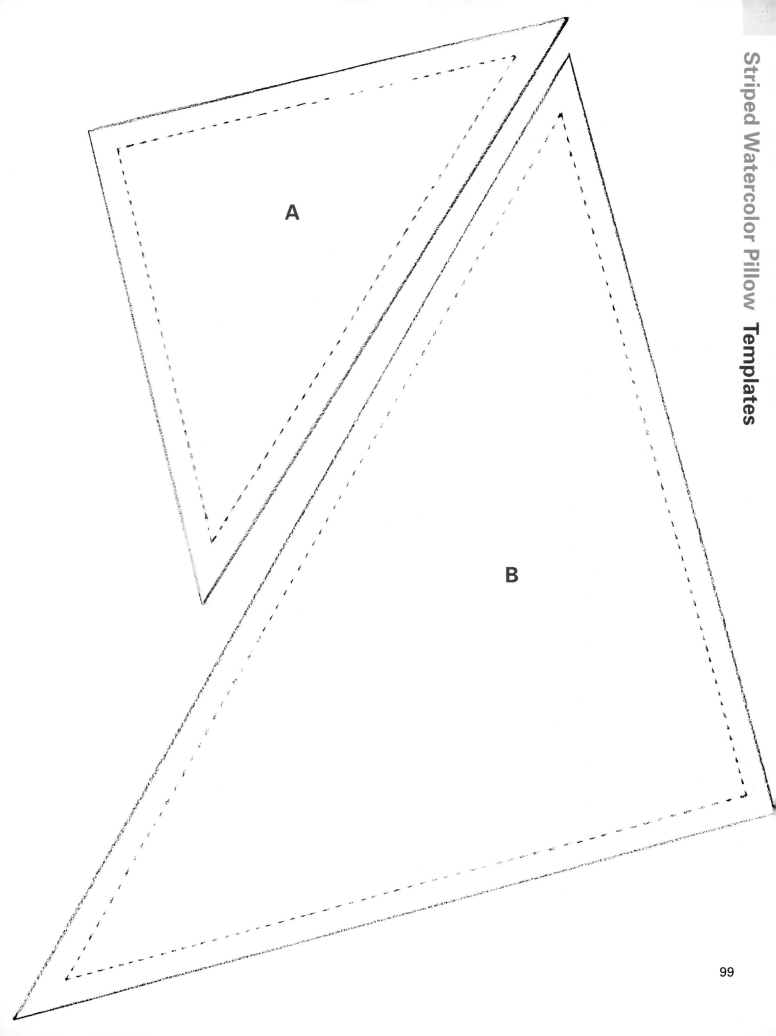

A

B

Harlequin Watercolor Pillow

The pattern of brightly colored diamond shapes got its name from the graphic costumes worn by comic entertainers called Harlequins. Although most often associated with French decoration, these diamonds are also popular in Asian design. The pattern is a checkerboard turned on its ear, which is then made more sophisticated with elongation. Shimmery bands of moiré fabric offset these orderly rows of blue and green diamonds.

FINISHED SIZE: 14" SQUARE ■ SEAM ALLOWANCES: ¼"

Materials Needed

¼-yard gold moiré fabric
¼-yard blue print cotton fabric
¼-yard green stain fabric
¼-yard melon cotton fabric
⅛-yard ivory cotton fabric
15" square cotton fabric (pillow back)
14" pillow form

Scraps of the following fabrics:
• cream print cotton
• wheat silk
• light blue cotton
Air-soluble marking pen
Tracing paper
Coordinating thread

Cutting Plan

1. With the tracing paper, make the templates from the originals found on page 103. Broken lines indicate seam lines.

2. Cut the following:
    *   3 $1\frac{7}{8}$" x 36" strips from the green satin
    * $1\frac{3}{8}$" x 15" strip from the green satin
    * $1\frac{3}{8}$" x 15" strip from the green satin
    *   2 2" x 42" strips from the blue cotton fabric
    * $3\frac{1}{4}$" x $7\frac{1}{2}$" rectangle from the gold moiré fabric
    * $9\frac{1}{4}$" x $3\frac{1}{4}$" rectangle from the gold moiré fabric
    * $4\frac{7}{8}$" x $3\frac{1}{4}$" rectangle from the gold moiré
    * $4\frac{7}{8}$" x $3\frac{1}{4}$" rectangle from the gold moiré
    *   2 "A" triangles from the light blue fabric
    *   2 "A" triangles from the blue print fabric
    * $6\frac{1}{2}$" x $3\frac{1}{4}$" rectangle from the wheat silk
    *   "B" triangle from the cream print fabric
    * $1\frac{3}{8}$" x 15" strip from the ivory fabric
    * $1\frac{3}{8}$" x 15" strip from the ivory fabric
    * $4\frac{7}{8}$" x $10\frac{1}{4}$" rectangle from the melon fabric
    * $4\frac{7}{8}$" x $10\frac{1}{4}$" rectangle from the melon fabric

Assembly

1. Alternating the $1\frac{7}{8}$" x 36" green satin strips with the blue cotton strips of the same size, stitch the strips together. Press.

2. Referring to Figure 4-9, mark the diagonal lines on the wrong side of the pieced section to make five strips. Position the lines to create diamonds that are $1\frac{1}{2}$" wide and $3\frac{3}{4}$" long.

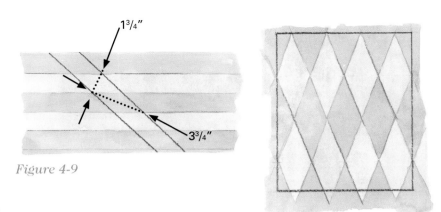

Figure 4-9

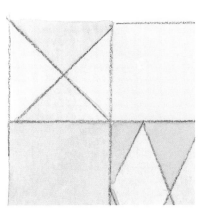

Figure 4-11

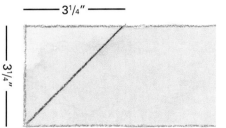

Figure 4-12

Figure 4-10

Figure 4-13

3. Stagger the strips to create a harlequin pattern, as shown in Figure 4-10. Stitch together to create a section that measures at least 6$\frac{1}{2}$" x 7$\frac{1}{2}$". Cut and stitch green triangles at the corners, if necessary. Press.

4. On the wrong side of the pieced section, align the tops and sides of the blue diamonds and draw a 6" x 7" rectangle. Mark the wrong side of the pieced section with the marking pen. Trim $\frac{1}{4}$" from the marked line.

5. Stitch the long side of the 3$\frac{1}{4}$" x 7$\frac{1}{2}$" gold moiré rectangle to the left side of the pieced section, as in Figure 4-11.

6. Alternating the two light blue "A" triangles with the two blue print "A" triangles, stitch the short sides of the triangles together to make a square measuring 3$\frac{1}{4}$". Press.

7. Stitch the pieced square to the short end of the 6$\frac{1}{2}$" x 3$\frac{1}{4}$" wheat silk rectangle. Press.

8. Stitch the pieced strip to the pieced section, as shown in Figure 4-12. Press.

9. Mark the wrong side of the 9$\frac{1}{4}$" x 3$\frac{1}{4}$" gold moiré rectangle with the marking pen, as in Figure 4-12, and trim $\frac{1}{4}$" from the marked line.

10. Matching the long side of the cream "B" triangle to the marked line, stitch together. Press.

11. Stitch the rectangle to the pieced section, as shown in Figure 4-13. Press.

12. Stitch together the long sides of the 1$\frac{3}{8}$" x 15" ivory strip to the green satin strip of the same size.

13. Perpendicular to the seam, cut nine $1\frac{3}{8}$"-wide rectangles from the ivory-green satin piece and stitch the short ends together to make one long strip. Press.

14. Stitch the ivory-green satin strip to the left side of the pieced section.

15. Stitch the long side of the $4\frac{7}{8}$" x $3\frac{1}{4}$" gold moiré rectangle to the short side of the $4\frac{7}{8}$" x $10\frac{1}{4}$" melon rectangle. Press.

16. With the gold moiré at the top, stitch the pieced rectangle to the left side of the pieced section to complete the square. Press.

Pillow Assembly

1. With the right sides together, pin the pillow front to the pillow back and stitch together, leaving a 7" opening on one side. Trim the excess fabric from the corners.

2. Turn right-side out, press, and insert the pillow form.

3. Whipstitch the opening closed.

Templates

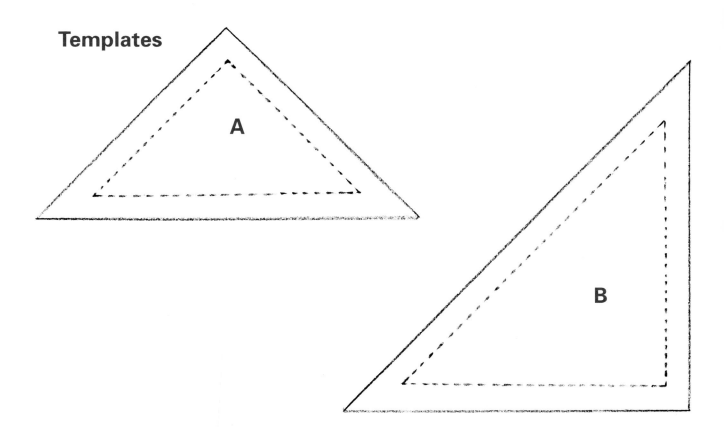

Ladder Watercolor Pillow

The narrow, checked borders on each side of the triangles suggest pieced ladders. The ladder has long been a metaphor for the means by which one attains eminence. Turn the pillow sideways, and the ascending and descending motion becomes static.

FINISHED SIZE: 14" SQUARE ■ SEAM ALLOWANCES: ¹/₄"

Materials Needed

$\frac{1}{4}$-yard tan print cotton fabric

$\frac{1}{8}$-yard gold textured silk fabric

$\frac{1}{8}$-yard wheat silk fabric

$\frac{1}{8}$-yard green silk fabric

$\frac{1}{8}$-yard light blue cotton fabric

15" square cotton fabric (pillow back)

14" pillow form

Coordinating thread

Large scraps of the following cotton fabrics:

- gray
- purple
- blue print
- cream print
- pink moiré

Air-soluble marking pen

Cutting Plan

1. With the tracing paper, make the templates from the originals found on page 107. Broken lines indicate seam lines.

2. Cut the following:
   - 2 $2\frac{7}{8}$" x $8\frac{3}{4}$" strips from the light blue fabric
   - $2\frac{7}{8}$" x $8\frac{3}{4}$" strip from the blue print fabric
   - 2 triangles from the light blue fabric
   - 3 $1\frac{1}{4}$" x $2\frac{1}{2}$" strips from the purple fabric
   - 2 $1\frac{1}{4}$" x $2\frac{1}{2}$" strips from the pink moiré fabric
   - $2\frac{1}{2}$" x $6\frac{3}{4}$" rectangle from the wheat silk
   - $5\frac{3}{8}$" x $3\frac{3}{4}$" rectangle from the cream print fabric
   - $6\frac{5}{8}$" x $10\frac{1}{2}$" rectangle from the tan print fabric
   - $6\frac{5}{8}$" x $3\frac{3}{4}$" rectangle from the gray fabric
   - $1\frac{1}{4}$" x $11\frac{1}{2}$" strip from the green silk
   - $3\frac{1}{2}$" x $14\frac{1}{2}$" rectangle from the gold textured silk

Assembly

1. Alternating the two 2⅞" x 8¾" light blue strips with the blue print strips of the same size, stitch the long sides of the strips together. Press.

2. Perpendicular to the seam, cut three 2⅞"-wide (and the length of the stitched piece) rectangles.

3. Stagger the rectangles to create a diamond pattern and stitch together.

4. Cut and stitch light blue triangles at the corners.

5. Align the sides of the diamonds, as in Figure 4-14, and with the air-soluble marking pen, draw a 3⅜" x 10" rectangle on the wrong side of the pieced section. Trim ¼" from the marked line.

6. Alternating the three 1¼" x 2½" purple strips with the pink moiré strips of the same size, stitch the long sides together.

7. Stitch the short side of the wheat silk rectangle to the long side of a purple strip. Press. Cut in half lengthwise.

8. Stitch one pieced strip to the long side of the diamond section. Rotate the second strip and stitch it to the opposite side of the diamond section. Press.

9. From the cream print fabric, cut one 5⅜" x 3¾" rectangle. Stitch the long side of the rectangle to the short side of the pieced section. Press.

10. Stitch the short side of 6⅝" x 10½" tan rectangle to the long side of 6⅝" x 3¾" gray rectangle.

11. Stitch the pieced rectangles to the diamond section, as shown in Figure 4-15. Press.

Figure 4-14

Figure 4-15

12. Stitch the 1¼" x 11½" green silk strip to the top of the pieced section.

13. Stitch the gold textured silk rectangle to the left side of the pieced section to complete the square.

Pillow Assembly

1. With the right sides together, pin the pillow front to the pillow back and stitch together, leaving a 7" opening on one side. Trim the excess fabric from the corners.

2. Turn right-side out, press, and insert the pillow form.

3. Whipstitch the opening closed.

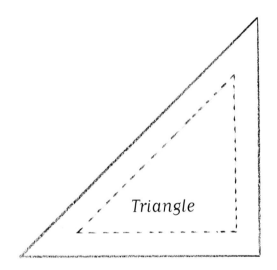

Triangle

Honeycomb Watercolor Pillow

When worked in light colors, the hexagon makes up a honeycomb pattern. When worked in dark colors, it is known as the tortoiseshell pattern, as with amber hexagons covering a shiny lacquered box.

FINISHED SIZE: 14" SQUARE ■ SEAM ALLOWANCES: ¼"

Materials Needed

$\frac{1}{8}$-yard gray cotton fabric

$\frac{1}{8}$-yard green silk fabric

$\frac{1}{8}$-yard pink moiré fabric

$\frac{1}{8}$-yard light green print fabric

$\frac{1}{8}$-yard violet metallic fabric

Tracing paper

Air-soluble marking pen

Coordinating thread

15" square cotton fabric (pillow back)

14" pillow form

Cutting Plan

1. With the tracing paper, make the templates from the originals found on page 111. Broken lines indicate seam lines. On the notched border template, fold the tracing paper at the broken line to make the template $13\frac{1}{4}$" long.

2. Cut the following, noting any referenced steps first, before cutting:
    *   6 hexagons from the pink moiré fabric (note Assembly step 1)
    *   2 $2\frac{3}{4}$" squares from the pink moiré fabric
    *   6 hexagons from the light green print fabric (note Assembly step 1)
    *   2 $2\frac{3}{4}$" squares from the green print fabric
    *   4 hexagons from the green silk (note Assembly step 1)
    * $2\frac{3}{4}$" square from the green silk
    *   3 hexagons from the violet metallic fabric (note Assembly step 1)
    * $2\frac{3}{4}$" square from the violet metallic fabric
    * $2\frac{1}{2}$" x $13\frac{3}{4}$" strip from the violet metallic fabric
    *   1 border shape from the gray cotton fabric (note Assembly step 4)
    *   2" x $13\frac{3}{4}$" strip from the gray cotton fabric
    * $1\frac{3}{8}$" x 15" strip from the ivory fabric
    * $1\frac{3}{8}$" x 15" strip from the green satin

Assembly

1. On the wrong side of the pink moiré, draw six hexagons with the air-soluble marking pen, allowing at least $\frac{1}{2}$" between each shape. Allowing $\frac{1}{4}$" around the marked lines when cutting out the shapes.

2. Repeat step 1 for the six light green print hexagons, four green silk hexagons, and three violet metallic hexagons.

3. Matching the marked lines on the sides of the hexagons, hand-stitch the shapes together in the sequence shown in Figure 4-16, making three rows of hexagons. Hand-stitch the rows together.

Figure 4-16

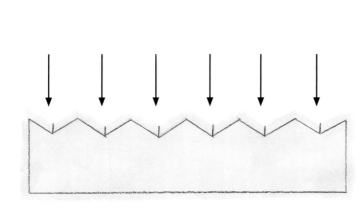

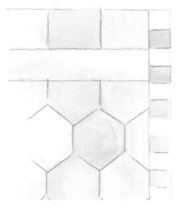

Figure 4-17
Figure 4-18

4. Draw the border shape on the gray fabric with the marking pen and allow $1/4$"
   around the marked line when cutting it out. Clip the fabric at the inside corners,
   as in Figure 4-17.

5. To inset the gray border, match the first side of one angle to the marked line of the
   first hexagon. Stitch to the clipped corner. Realign the pieces and stitch the adjoining
   side of the angle to the remaining line of the hexagon. Continue to stitch the border
   to the top row of hexagons. Press.

6. With the marking pen, mark the wrong side of the bottom row of hexagons to make
   it flush. Trim $1/4$" from the marked line.

7. Stitch the 2" x $13^3/_4$" gray cotton strip to the bottom row of hexagons.

8. Stitch the $2^3/_4$" pink, green print, green silk, and violet squares together in the same
   sequence as the bottom row of hexagons. Press.

9. Stitch the pieced squares to the gray strip. Press.

10. Stitch the $2^1/_2$" x $13^3/_4$" violet metallic strip to the notched border. Press.

11. Stitch together the long sides of the $1^3/_8$" x 15" ivory and green satin strips.

12. Perpendicular to the seam, cut nine $1^3/_8$"-wide ivory-green satin rectangles.

13. Stitch the short ends of the nine ivory-green satin pieces together to make one long
    strip. Press.

14. Stitch the ivory-green satin strip to the left side of the pieced section, as shown in
    Figure 4-18. Press.

Pillow Assembly

1. With the right sides together, pin the pillow front to the pillow back and stitch
   together, leaving a 7" opening on one side. Trim the excess fabric from the corners.

2. Turn right-side out, press, and insert the pillow form.

3. Whipstitch the opening closed.

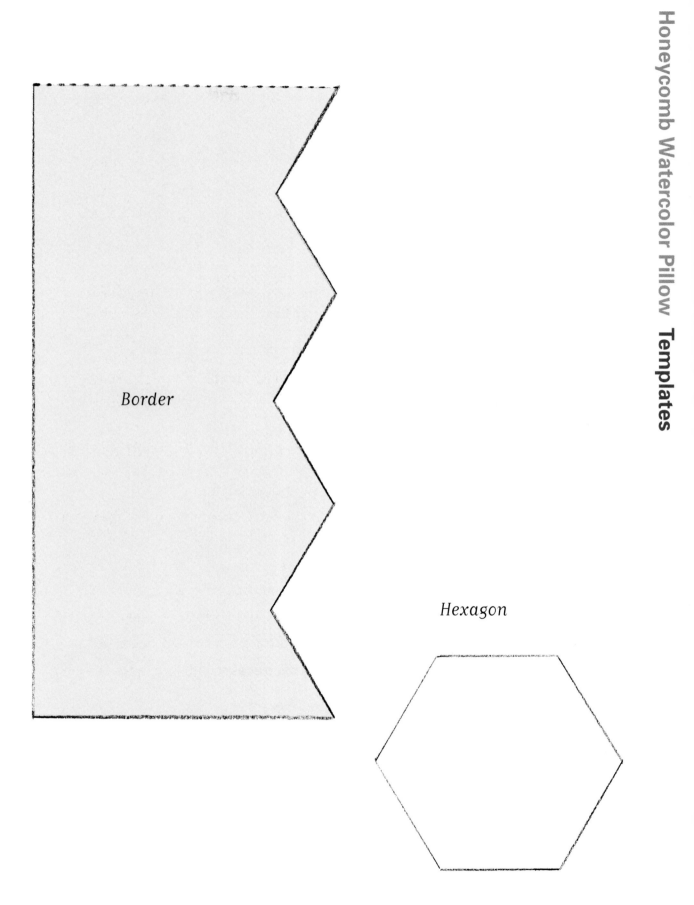

Border

Hexagon

Scrolls

"To have little is to possess.
To have plenty is to be
perplexed."
—Lao-Tzu, 604-531 BC

Clutter is regarded to be intrusive and therefore is discouraged. Accessories are carefully selected in accordance to the season.

Those possessions not on display are carefully stored in specially made boxes. Scroll painting was inspired by literature to illustrate historical narratives and fanciful stories. Vertical scrolls show single depictions and are hung from a slim rod affixed to the top edge, while horizontal scrolls have successive illustrations and have rods at each end. They are unrolled and read from right to left. While horizontal scrolls are most often stored in special boxes, vertical scrolls are displayed on the wall and have become the epitome of the Asian art form.

Traditionally hung on the walls of tearooms, scrolls today are suitable for use in tall spaces such as entries and stairwells. The techniques used to make these scrolls dictate that they be made from fabric rather than paper so the style is simpler and more graphic. The feel and the format, however, remain the same.

Fan Scroll

Statements are made in Japanese interiors with a strong exclamation point of color or shape. Both color and shape punctuate this scroll—the magenta dye and the fan silhouette.

FINISHED SIZE: 14 1/2" X 33" ■ SEAM ALLOWANCES: 1/4"

Materials Needed

$\frac{1}{2}$-yard ivory print cotton fabric

$\frac{1}{3}$-yard burgundy cotton fabric

$\frac{1}{8}$-yard gold cotton fabric

$\frac{1}{2}$-yard cotton fabric for backing

Large scrap of dark green print (appliqué)

Large scrap of floral fabric (appliqué)

Matching threads for appliqué

Coordinating thread for assembly

Tracing paper

Air-soluble marking pen

Pink thread for machine embroidery

Cream thread

Magenta cold-water dye

$\frac{5}{8}$"-diameter wooden dowel

Green or gray acrylic paint (optional)

24" piece cream pearl cotton

Cutting Plan

1. With the tracing paper, make the template from the original found on page 118. Broken lines indicate seam lines.

2. Cut the following, noting any referenced steps first, before cutting:
   - 12" x 16" rectangle from the ivory fabric
   - 16" x 9" rectangle from the ivory fabric
   - $4\frac{1}{4}$" x $14\frac{1}{2}$" rectangle from the ivory fabric
   - 15" x $11\frac{1}{2}$" rectangle from the burgundy fabric
   - 2 $1\frac{3}{8}$" x $14\frac{1}{2}$" strips from the burgundy fabric
   - 1 fan shape from the floral fabric (note Appliqué step 1)
   - 1 arc shape from the dark green print fabric (note Appliqué step 3)
   - 2 1" x $14\frac{1}{2}$" strips from the gold fabric.
   - 2 $4\frac{1}{2}$" x $14\frac{1}{2}$" rectangles from the vertical dyed rectangle
   - 15" x $33\frac{1}{2}$" rectangle from the backing fabric

Fold the rectangle accordion-style in the dish.

Hold the dyed fabric piece over the dish or sink to allow the excess to drip off.

Place the dyed fabric on paper towels to dry.

Fabric Dyeing

1. Immerse the 12" x 16" ivory rectangle fabric in cold water and blot.

2. Following the manufacturer's directions, mix the dye in a shallow glass dish.

3. Hold the vertical rectangle at the top corners and dip the rectangle in the dye, folding it accordion-style in the dish, as shown above left. Do not immerse the entire piece in the dye. The premoistened fabric will allow the dye to bleed up through the ivory threads and create an irregular blended line.

4. When the desired dye pattern is achieved, remove the fabric from the dye and hold it over the dish or the sink as the excess dye drips from the bottom edge, as shown above center.

5. Place the rectangle flat on several layers of paper towels, as shown above right. Don't fold the fabric onto itself as the dye will leach through. Let dry. Press.

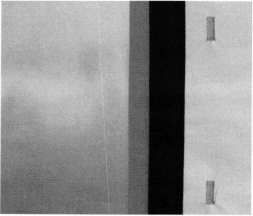

6. Repeat steps 1 through 4 with the 16" x 9" ivory rectangle.

7. Hand-launder the fabric to remove excess dye. When the fabric is dry, it will be two to three shades lighter than it was when wet, as shown at right.

The dry fabric will be two to three shades lighter than how it when it was wet.

Appliqué

1. On the right side of the floral fabric, draw the fan shape with the air-soluble marking pen. Referring to the Needle-Turned Appliqué instructions on page 9, allow $\frac{1}{8}$" to $\frac{1}{4}$" around the marked line when cutting the shape.

2. Center the floral fan shape on the 15" x 11$\frac{1}{2}$" burgundy rectangle, pin in place, and hand-appliqué the fan shape to the rectangle.

3. On the right side of the dark green print fabric, draw the arc shape with the marking pen before cutting.

4. Position the arc shape on top of the fan, pin in place, and hand-appliqué the arc shape to the rectangle.

Scroll Assembly

1. Stitch the two 1$\frac{3}{8}$" x 14$\frac{1}{2}$" burgundy strips to the sides of the 4$\frac{1}{4}$" x 14$\frac{1}{2}$" ivory rectangle.

2. Stitch the two 1" x 14$\frac{1}{2}$" gold strips to the sides of the burgundy strips.

3. Stitch the two 4$\frac{1}{2}$" x 14$\frac{1}{2}$" vertical dyed rectangles to the sides of the gold strips. Press.

4. Stitch the pieced section to the appliquéd rectangle. Press.

5. Trim the horizontal dyed rectangle to 15" x 8$\frac{1}{2}$" and stitch it to the appliquéd rectangle. Press.

6. With the right sides together, pin the scroll front to the 15" x 33$\frac{1}{2}$" scroll back and stitch together, leaving a 5" opening on the bottom edge. Trim the excess fabric from the corners.

7. Turn right-side out. Press.

8. Whipstitch the opening closed.

9. Referring to Figure 5-1, use the marking pen to draw the dashes on the center ivory rectangle. Note that they are lightly offset and are aligned with the right seam.

10. On a scrap of fabric, satin stitch a short straight line by machine. Adjust your machine to the desired line width and coverage (the width of the dashes on the photo model is $\frac{3}{16}$"). With the pink thread, machine-stitch the dashes, as shown at right. Trim the thread ends.

11. Cut the dowel to 14$\frac{1}{2}$". Paint, if desired.

12. Place the scroll right-side down on the work surface. Place the dowel along the top edge of the scroll.

13. With the cream thread, stitch the dowel to the scroll at each end using several snug loops as stitches. Stitch at two additional points, 4" from each end.

14. From the pearl cotton, cut one 24" length, wrap the ends of the pearl cotton around the ends of the dowel, knot the pearl cotton, and trim the ends.

Figure 5-1

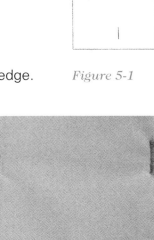

Machine-stitch the pink dashes.

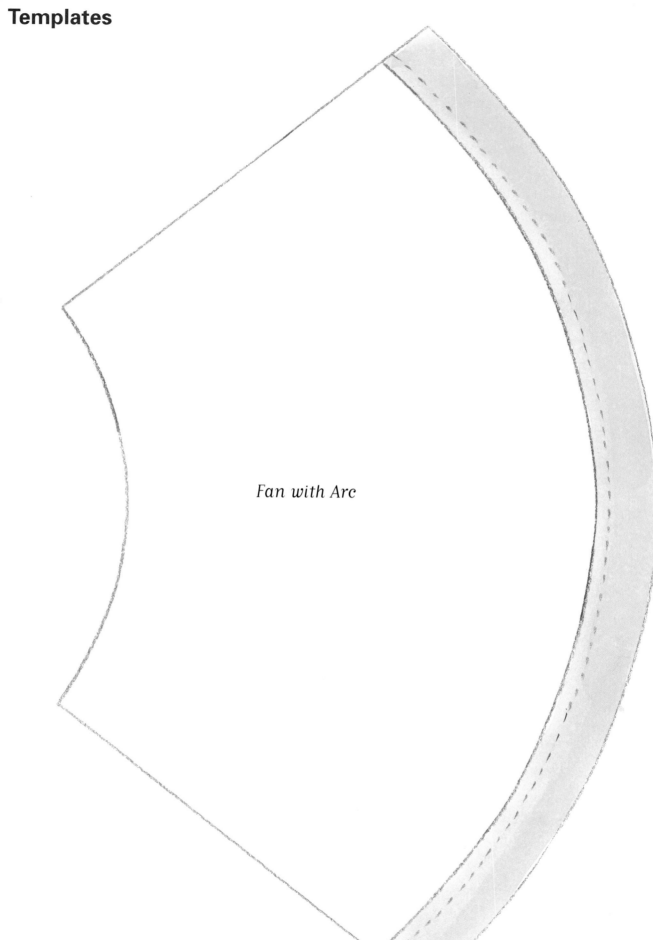

Fan with Arc

Peace Scroll

The gentle undulating edge of this dip-dyed fabric brings to mind painted rice paper. The fibers in rice paper are very porous and when paint is applied, it spreads throughout the fibers to create a beautiful soft edge.

FINISHED SIZE: 14½" X 33" ■ SEAM ALLOWANCES: ¼"

Materials Needed

½-yard ivory print cotton fabric

½-yard cotton fabric (backing)

¼-yard teal print cotton fabric

Large scraps of the following cotton fabrics (appliqué):

- dark green print
- light green print
- brown
- dark blue print

Matching threads for appliqué

Coordinating thread for assembly

Tracing paper

Air-soluble marking pen

Cream thread

Violet cold-water dye

⅝"-diameter wooden dowel

Green or gray acrylic paint (optional)

24" piece cream pearl cotton

Cutting Plan

1. With the tracing paper, make the templates from the originals found on pages 122 through 124. Broken lines indicate seam lines.

2. Cut the following, noting any referenced steps first, before cutting:
   - 15" x 35" rectangle from the ivory fabric
   - 2 triangles from the ivory print fabric
   - 1 peace symbol from the brown fabric (note Applique step 4)
   - 1 double-leaf shape from the light green print fabric
   - 1 single-leaf shape from the dark green print fabric
   - 1 set family symbols from the dark blue fabric
   - 2 1¼" x 15" strips from the teal print fabric
   - 2 1¼" x 33½" strips from the teal print fabric
   - 15" x 33½" rectangle from the backing fabric

Fabric Dyeing

1. Immerse the 15" x 35" ivory rectangle in cold water and blot.

2. Following the manufacturer's directions, mix the dye in a shallow glass dish.

3. Hold the ivory rectangle at the top corners and dip the rectangle in the dye, folding it accordion style in the dish. Do not immerse the entire piece in the dye. The premoistened fabric will allow the dye to bleed up through the ivory threads and create an irregular blended line.

4. When the desired dye pattern is achieved, remove the fabric from the dye and hold it over the dish or the sink as the excess dye drips from the bottom edge.

Tip: If further instruction is needed for Fabric Dyeing steps 1 through 5, beginning at left, refer back to the same steps in the Fan Scroll project, page 116, for step-by-step photos.

5. Place the rectangle flat on several layers of paper towels. Don't fold the fabric over on itself or the dye will leach through. Let dry. Press.

6. Hand-launder the fabric to remove excess dye. When the fabric is dry, it will be two or three shades lighter than it was when wet.

Appliqué

1. Referring to Figure 5-2, mark diagonal lines on the top corners of the wrong side of the dyed rectangle. Trim ¼" from the marked lines.

2. Stitch the long sides of two ivory print triangles to the marked lines. Press.

3. Trim the dyed rectangle to 13½" x 32".

4. Draw the shape on the fabric with the air-soluble marking pen. Referring to the Needle-Turned Appliqué instructions on page 9, allow ⅛" to ¼" around the marked line when cutting out the shape.

5. Center the brown shape on the dyed rectangle, pin in place, and hand-appliqué it to the rectangle.

6. Centering the light green double-leaf shape between the left and the right edge of the rectangle, and allowing approximately 4½" between the bottom of the leaves and the peace symbol, pin the shape to the rectangle. Hand-appliqué the double-leaf to the rectangle.

7. Center the dark green leaf on the light green double-leaf, pin in place, and hand-appliqué the leaf to the rectangle.

8. Centering the dark blue family symbols between the left and the right edge of the rectangle, and allowing approximately 4" between the bottom of the family symbol and the top circle of the family symbol, pin the dark blue pieces to the rectangle and hand-appliqué them in place.

Scroll Assembly

1. Center and stitch the two 1¼" x 15" teal strips to the top and the bottom of the appliquéd rectangle.

2. Center and stitch the two 1¼" x 33½" teal strips to the sides of the appliquéd rectangle.

3. Miter the corners, as instructed on page 7. Press.

The dry fabric is two to three shades lighter than it appeared when wet.

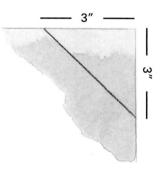

Figure 5-2

4. With the right sides together, pin the scroll front to the 15" x 33$\frac{1}{4}$" backing piece and stitch together, leaving a 5" opening on the bottom edge. Trim the excess fabric from the corners.

5. Turn right-side out. Press.

6. Whipstitch the opening closed.

7. Cut the dowel to 14$\frac{1}{2}$". Paint, if desired.

8. Place the scroll right-side down on the work surface. Place the dowel along the top edge of the scroll.

9. With the cream thread, stitch the dowel to the scroll at each end using several snug loops as stitches. Stitch at two additional points, 4" from each end.

10. From the pearl cotton, cut one 24" length, wrap the ends of the pearl cotton around the ends of the dowel, knot the pearl cotton, and trim the ends.

Templates

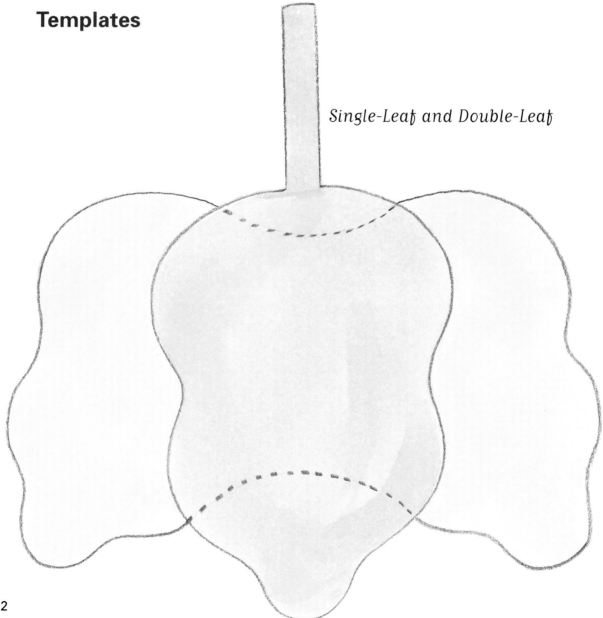

Single-Leaf and Double-Leaf

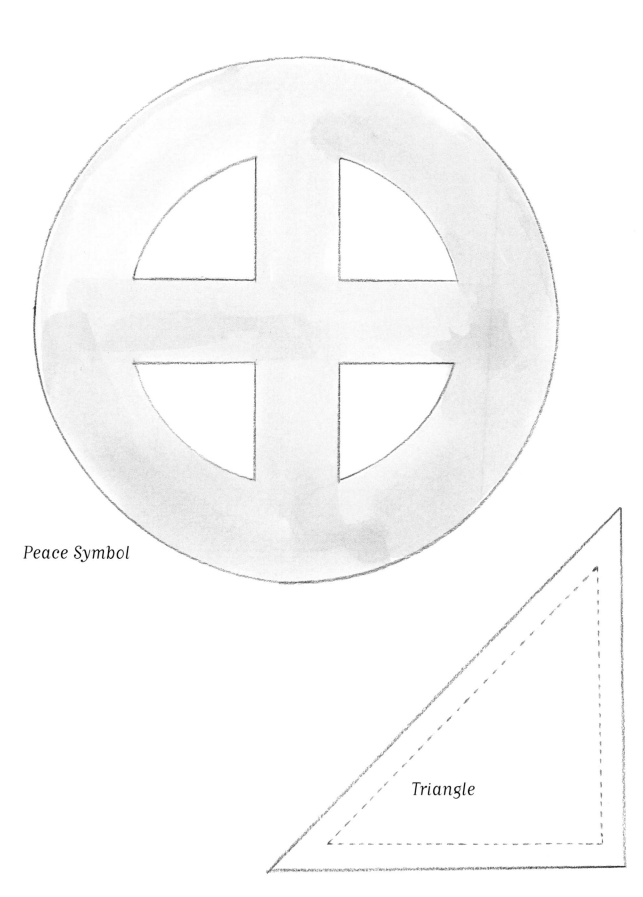

Peace Symbol

Triangle

Templates

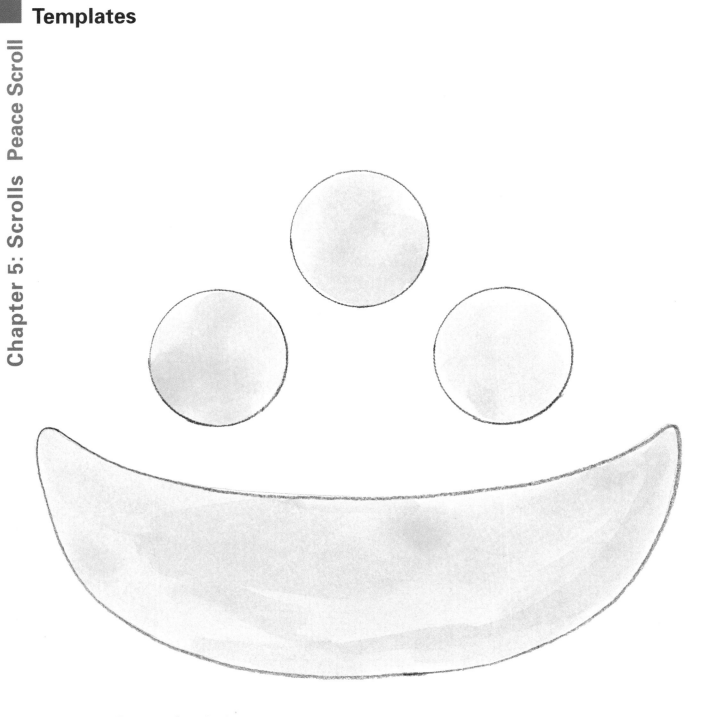

Family Symbol

Falling Leaves Scroll

Unfurl this scroll and display it when the heady days of summer turn to the crisp clear days of fall. The narrow stems of the leaves make this appliqué project an intermediate to advanced project.

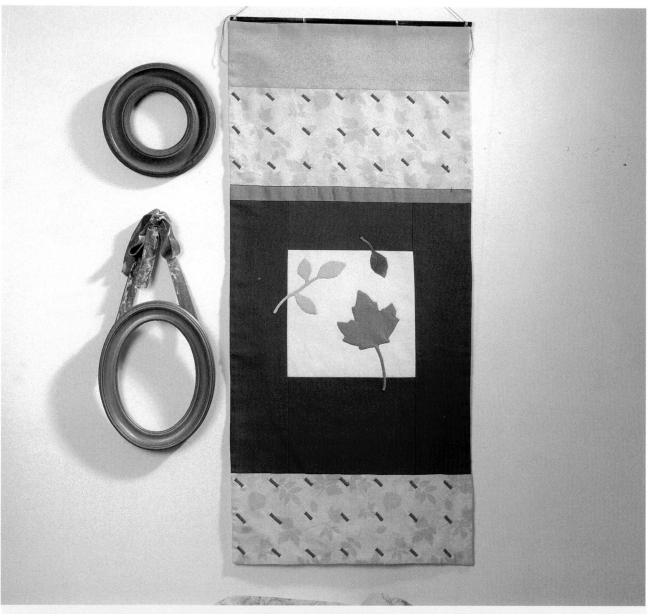

FINISHED SIZE: 14¹/₂" X 33" ■ SEAM ALLOWANCES: ¹/₄"

Materials Needed

$1/2$-yard burgundy cotton fabric

$1/4$-yard ivory print cotton fabric

$1/4$-yard light gold print cotton fabric

$1/4$-yard dark gold cotton fabric

$1/8$-yard brown cotton fabric

Scraps of the following cotton fabrics (appliqué)

- gray
- green print
- brown

Matching threads for appliqué

Coordinating thread for assembly

Tracing paper

Air-soluble marking pen

Orange thread

Cream thread

Violet cold-water dye

$5/8$"-diameter wooden dowel

Green or gray acrylic paint (optional)

24" piece gold pearl cotton

Cutting Plan

1. With the tracing paper, make the templates from the originals found on page 128. Broken lines indicate seam lines.

2. Cut the following, noting any referenced steps first, before cutting:
   - 8" square from the ivory print fabric
   - 8" x $3^1/_2$" rectangle from the burgundy fabric
   - 8" x $6^1/_2$" rectangle from the burgundy fabric
   - 2 4" x 17" strips from the burgundy fabric
   - $1^1/_2$" x 15" strip from the brown fabric
   - 2 15" x $6^1/_4$" rectangles from the light gold print fabric
   - 15" x $4^1/_2$" rectangle from the dark gold fabric
   - 1 small leaf from the green print fabric (note Appliqué step 1)
   - 1 medium leaf from the gray fabric (note Appliqué step 1)
   - 1 large leaf from the brown fabric (note Appliqué step 1)
   - 15" x $33^1/_2$" rectangle from the backing fabric

Assembly

1. Stitch the 8" x $3^1/_2$" burgundy rectangle to the top of the 8″ ivory square and the 8" x $6^1/_2$" burgundy rectangle to the bottom of the square. Press.

2. Stitch the two 4" x 17" burgundy strips to the sides of the pieced section. Press.

3. Stitch the $1^1/_2$" x 15" brown strip to the top of the pieced section.

4. Stitch the 15" x $6^1/_4$" light gold print rectangles to the top and the bottom of the pieced section.

5. Stitch the 15" x $4^1/_2$" dark gold rectangle to the top of the pieced section. Press.

Appliqué

1. On the right side of the green print fabric, draw the small leaf with the air-soluble marking pen. Refer to the Needle-Turned Appliqué instructions on page 9, allowing $1/8$" to $1/4$" around the marked line when cutting. Do the same for the medium leaf on the gray fabric and the large leaf on the brown fabric.

2. Referring to Figure 5-3 for placement, pin the green leaf in place and hand-appliqué it to the scroll.

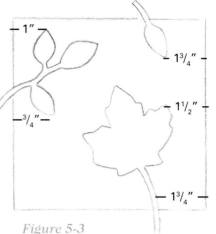

Figure 5-3

3. Pin the gray leaf shape in place and hand-appliqué it to the scroll.

4. Pin the brown leaf shape in place and hand-appliqué it to the scroll.

Scroll Assembly

1. With the right sides together, pin the scroll front to the 15" x $33 1/2$" backing piece. Stitch together, leaving a 5" opening on the bottom edge. Trim the excess fabric from the corners.

Figure 5-4

2. Turn right-side out. Press.

3. Whipstitch the opening closed.

4. Referring to Figure 5-4, use the marking pen to draw the dashes on the light gold print rectangles.

5. On a scrap of fabric, satin stitch a short straight line by machine. Adjust your machine to the desired line width and coverage. The width of the dashes on the photo model is $3/16$".

6. With the orange thread, machine stitch the dashes. Trim the thread ends.

7. Cut the dowel to $14 1/2$". Paint, if desired.

8. Place the scroll right-side down on the work surface. Place the dowel along the top edge of the scroll.

9. With the cream thread, stitch the dowel to the scroll at each end using several snug loops as stitches. Stitch at two additional points, 4" from each end.

10. From the pearl cotton, cut one 24" length, wrap the ends of the pearl cotton around the ends of the dowel, knot the pearl cotton, and trim the ends.

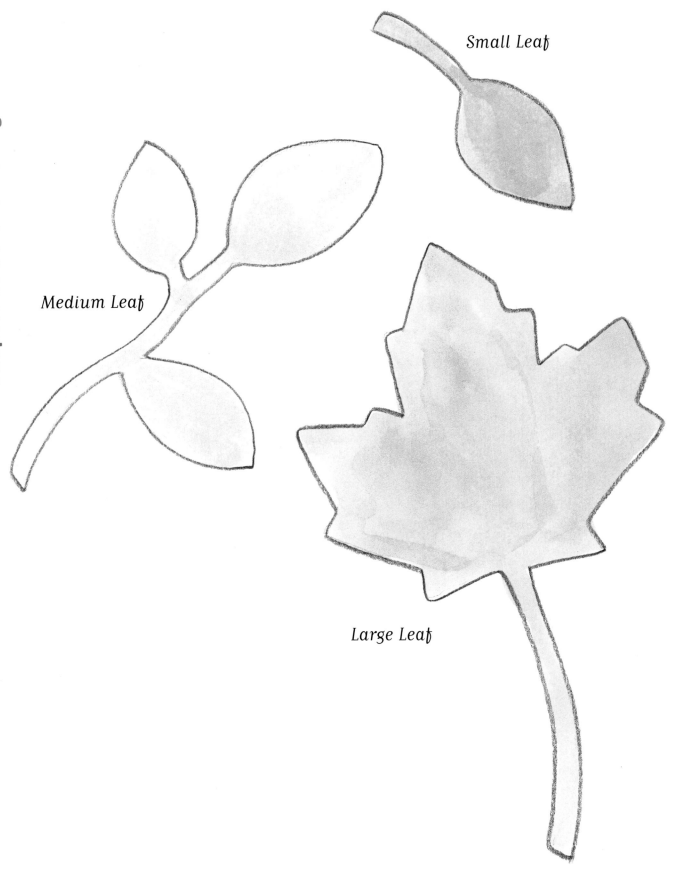

Small Leaf

Medium Leaf

Large Leaf